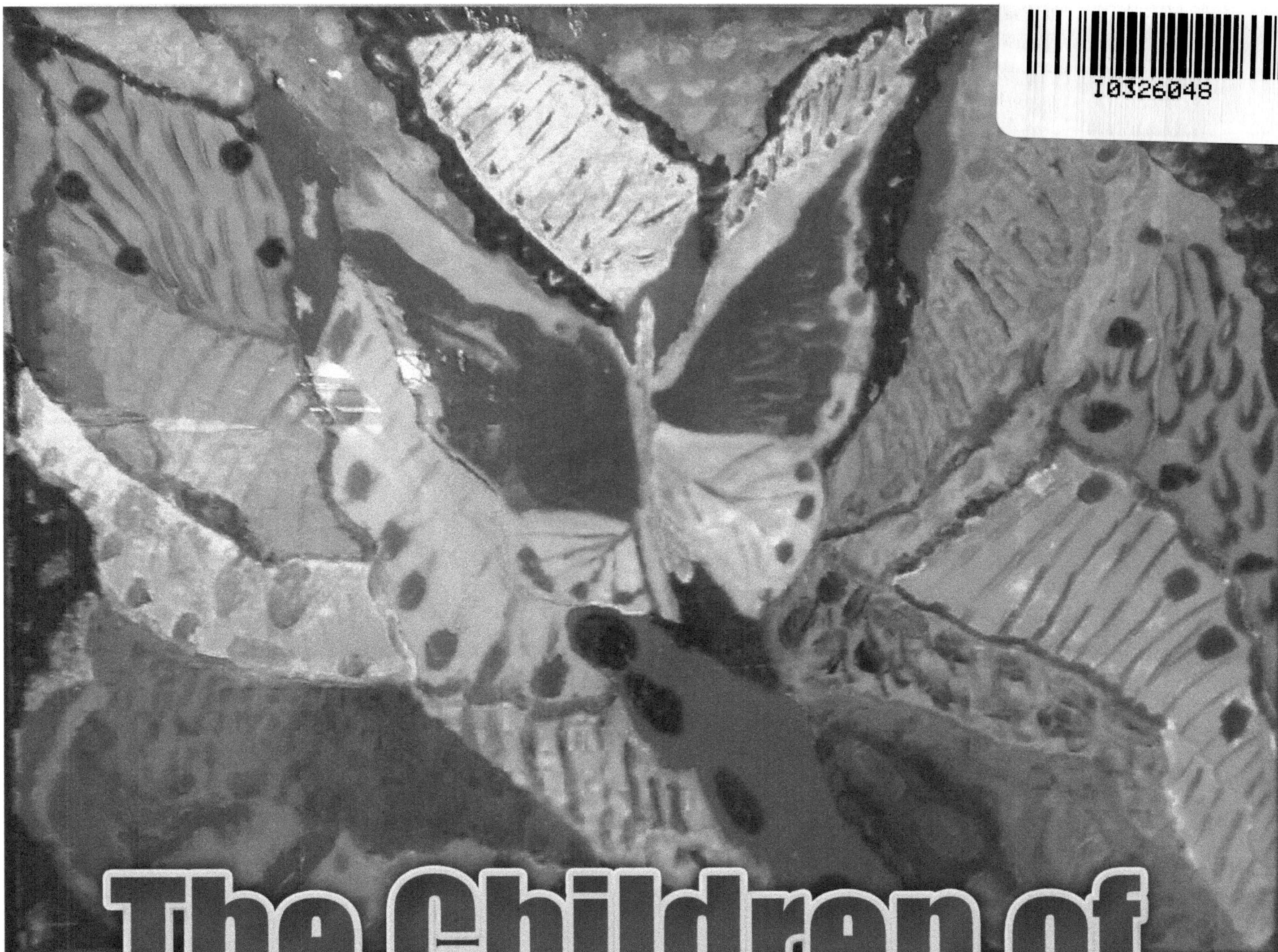

The Children of Ruth

A DOCUMENTARY THAT CHRONICLES THE MOBILIZATION AND METAMORPHOSIS OF A PEOPLE FROM MADISON COUNTY, TENNESSEE TO DEKALB, TEXAS

Written by:
Mattie Shavers Johnson

I0326048

Copyright © 2015 Mattie Shavers Johnson

No part of this book may be reproduced or transmitted in any form or by any means, graphic, electronic, or mechanical, including photocopying, recording, taping, or by any information storage retrieval system, without the permission, in writing, of the publisher or author.

Lowbar Publishing Company
905 S. Douglas Ave.
Nashville, Tennessee 37204
615-972-2842
E-mail: Lowbarpublishingcompany@gmail.com
Web site: www.Lowbarbookstore.com

Scripture references in this book are taken from the King James Version (KJV) of the Holy Bible, unless otherwise noted.

Printed in the United States of America

Editor: Audrey Hall and Wendy Williams
Graphic and cover design artist: Norah S. Branch

ISBN:

For additional information, speaking engagements and details on workshops and seminars, contact the author:
Mattie Shavers Johnson
Nashville, Tennessee
Lowbarpublishingcompany@gmail.com

The Children of Ruth

TIME REFERENCE:
1836 – BONDAGE IN TEXAS
JUNE 1865 (JUNETEENTH)

THE CHILDREN OF RUTH

A DOCUMENTARY CHRONICLING THE MOBILIZATION AND METAMORPHOSIS OF A PEOPLE FROM MADISON COUNTY, TENNESSEE TO DEKALB, TEXAS
1848 -1858 AND BEYOND

Written by Mattie Shavers Johnson

With: Iverson E. Shavers (Lt. Col. Ret)
Raynard Kington
Jenna Shavers Benton

Other Contributors
Myrtle S. Downs
Mildred S. Kington
Livette S. Johnson
Charles W. Johnson, Jr.
Bessie Merle Garland Singleton
Thelma Rae Swink King
Stanley Shavers
Geneva Hubbard Bizzell
And daughter Gen (Geneva)

CONTENTS

ABOUT THE BOOK:

This book represents a sampling of how many communities through America were founded by descendants of slaves, slave masters and some of the slave master's children; and also other slaves bought from other states and nations in the world (mostly Africa). These slaves developed a social economic cultural, religious life that rivals any nation or people. It documents their experiences and represents a continuum of determined people to survive in a hostile and changing environment in the total world.

A great portion of the information for this book grew out of history passed on to the grandchildren by James P. Garland and by his daughter, Laura Garland, and her husband, Robert Shavers. Our mother, Laura Garland Shavers, talked to us often about our heritage although we forgot most of it. However, by pounding it in from time to time some of it stuck. My mother kept a pillowcase filled with photographs in a closet behind a bed or in some other place where she could retrieve the pictures. Most of the pictures were large and were pictures of her teacher, pastor, father, grandmother, aunts, cousins, sisters, or brother. Consequently, we were able to hold onto many family photographs. No one ever saw a picture of her mother, Jennie; however, some letters which were written to my mother in later years, detailed to some extent how my grandmother looked.

At the time of the writing of this book, most of the third generation of Garlands (my aunts and uncles) had passed. It has been difficult to contact or obtain information from most members of the fourth and fifth generation; many did not even own a picture of their parents or their siblings. Only two from the fifth generation contributed what they remembered or were told or had pictures to share. Hopefully, upon reading this book, other Garland family members, even those whose memories to this point have been stymied, will be able to summon up meaningful recollections from their personal past in the form of oral histories recalled or actual events which occurred during their lifetimes. Also, it is hoped that this text may be useful to unrelated members of the Garland Community who may be able to find a context for understanding and remembering their own related past.

MOBILIZATION

Mobilization (travel) during the middle of the eighteen hundreds was a great challenge for any individual or group. It was exceptionally difficult when there were no paved roads, money to advance a vehicle for travel or technology to create it for a vehicle of comfort or speed. With the extra problem of inclement weather, (rain, sleet, snow) the challenge could be even worse.

The almanac shows the possibility of inclement weather during fall (after crops were gathered). Indeed, slaves and their master encountered such challenges moving from Madison County, Tennessee to Texas.

ART

COVER: BY MATTIE S. JOHNSON (OIL ON CANVAS)
PENCIL DRAWING - MOBILIZATION AND METAMORPHOSIS OF A PEOPLE

...BY PHILLIP N. JOHNSON

MOBILIZATION AND METAMORPHOSIS OF A PEOPLE

TILLING AND PLANTING IMAGE

BUTTERFLY ART
METAMORPHOSIS IMAGE

STATEMENT

{Inspired by <u>Hamlet</u>, by William Shakespeare}

No matter how the log is hewn,
There is divinity in its
destiny.

Ruth Garland

1818-1903

Ruth Garland's Children

{As Listed by Laura Garland Shavers, 3rd generation-
Daughter of James Polk Garland; Ruth's son}

Emmaline Garland Frier
Sarah Garland Garland (slave Garland)
Dolly Garland Swink
James Polk Garland
Raimie Garland Holt
Emma Garland Robinson
Eliza (or Elsie) Garland Haynes
Robert Garland
Lee Garland
Tennessee Garland King
Mary Garland Johnson
Jane Garland Waller
Others may have died in child birth - (Charlie)
Jack Garland – [Son of James (Jim) Garland before
marriage to Ruth]

THE CHILDREN OF RUTH

{As Listed by Laura Garland Shavers, 3rd generation-
Daughter of James Polk Garland; Ruth's son}

Dollie Garland Swink

James Polk Garland

Tennessee Garland King

Robert Garland

EXCERPT FROM:

"The First Pip"

By:

Mattie S. Johnson

They had heard the
thunderous sound
like an egg-chick pipping
its passion
Forward to the sun;
Through the tunnel it comes
Wet with the embers
of indignation;
Striking the door of
early morning
with hammers of the
universe;
To be blown dry
by the sanctity of
the wind.

DEDICATION

This book is dedicated to the descendants of Ruth Garland, six and seven generations who can take pride in the love and care concerning their heritage, and to those who became seekers of freedom from the bonds of slavery and who worked tirelessly to bring freedom to reality for all people.

This book is also dedicated to the memory of Ruth Garland, referred to as the matriarch of Garland Community after slavery. She was an indentured servant though not recognized as a slave, for she was the daughter of a slave owner. She had privileges that other slaves did not have, yet, because she was a female, she was denied other privileges. Even today, certain cultures deem women as inferior, without certain rights. During ancient times, the Bible speaks of women as chattel and as being unclean at certain times of the month and after childbirth. This was true of Mary Magdalene who was involved in a sexual encounter. She alone was abandoned by society even though the male counterpart was as much to blame as she. Jesus Christ, a man of compassion, came to her rescue and asked her to "Go and sin no more."

Biblical history records that Mary Magdalene moved among the disenfranchised the sick, the weak, and the deprived. She was with Jesus at the cross and during the discovery of the empty tomb and the disclosure of him being resurrected. Today there are many Mary Magdalenes. As Ruth and her female descendants carry the cross of many and obey the teachings of Christ, they deserve to be honored and forgiven for their sins.

PREFACE

Storytelling to document facts has been one of the greatest gifts Africans and Americans of African descent have had since the advent of communication. It was and still is one of the ways to keep African history alive during the early centuries and even today. This skill was almost always designated to the "guru" or oldest, most senior citizen in a community or tribe. He or she could recite genealogy twenty to fifty years before or even longer. This gift of memory was passed on to the youngest and brightest member of the "guru's" family.

In our quest to keep history alive, recordings are now either written, spoken, placed on a disk or a chip, or labeled and stored in archives to be retrieved by the public when the subject needs investigating. It is a necessary tool for measuring mobility of a nation from whence it has come and may demonstrate where they are set to go.

Introduction

It has been said "change is the only event that is constant in this universe." It is inevitable. Birds still fly south just before winter and back again when spring is on the horizon. We always look for the October interlude of beautiful leaves, the "changing of the green," the metamorphosis of the butterfly; and so it is with mankind, always searching, looking for a better place to improve his plight in life, transferring from caterpillar to butterfly. It was apparent before the advent of the slavery of men and will continue until the end of time, as we know it. Thus, it was during the latter part of eighteen forty-eight (1848) or the eighteen fifties (1850's) when Col. John Garland decided to move his family from Madison County Tennessee to DeKalb, Texas. This book is about one family and its metamorphosis.

Chapter 1

THE JOURNEY

DeKalb and Location

DeKalb, Texas is a town located between Texarkana and Clarksville, Texas; 12 miles from the border of Oklahoma, with a population of approximately 1900-2000 inhabitants. The Garland community is located in this area one and a half to two miles west of DeKalb. It is now listed on the National Register of Historic Places.

This is where John C. Garland chose to locate and establish a plantation, an area that covers between six to seven thousand acres of land that had been claimed by other settlers before the Civil War. It was granted and sold as unsettled land. Some portions of this land were where "squatters" located.

Records in Bowie County, New Boston, Texas show that John Garland owned 27 slaves. Their names, ages, places of origin, and heritage are listed in the appendix.

John Garland's marker or tombstone is located in Annona, Texas which refers to him as *Colonel John C. Garland.* His grandfather had served in other wars; the Confederate or the Spanish American War; General Grant was his fourth cousin. He was a descendent of high ranking soldiers. Some of his relatives can be traced back to the 6th century in England.

(Vanderbilt University Library Archives).

The 30/49 Connection

There is a place where two major roads meet; it has been known as the **30/49 Connection** *(*now called the Regional Economic Group). In this place, business thrives; a strong transportation network keeps supply chains open and products moving to the customer. Here, the four corners of Texas, Arkansas, Louisiana and Oklahoma meet. It is the graphic center of North America. All routes identified **as** NAFTA corridors pass through this region. The majority of the continent's imports and exports pass through the **30/49 Connection**, serving all domestic and international markets. The transportation network in this area includes over 15 well-maintained interstate and highway systems transecting the region. Because of this fact, all major freight companies have terminals here and a Foreign Trade Zone has been established in Northeast Texas. In the midst of all this lies the Garland Community in DeKalb, Texas.

Cotton Field of James Hughes Farm Brownsville, Tennessee

Taken 10-26-13

THE JOURNEY

Essence of a Force

Asleep in each cocoon
we beat
The essence of a force,
and there,
In planned grace
We seek
A fortune left; our bread
We take,
Each day before the sun we make
Another try at the door,
As we strive to open it once more
To take our ordered
Place for flight.

MAP SHOWING LOCATION OF DEKALB, TEXAS

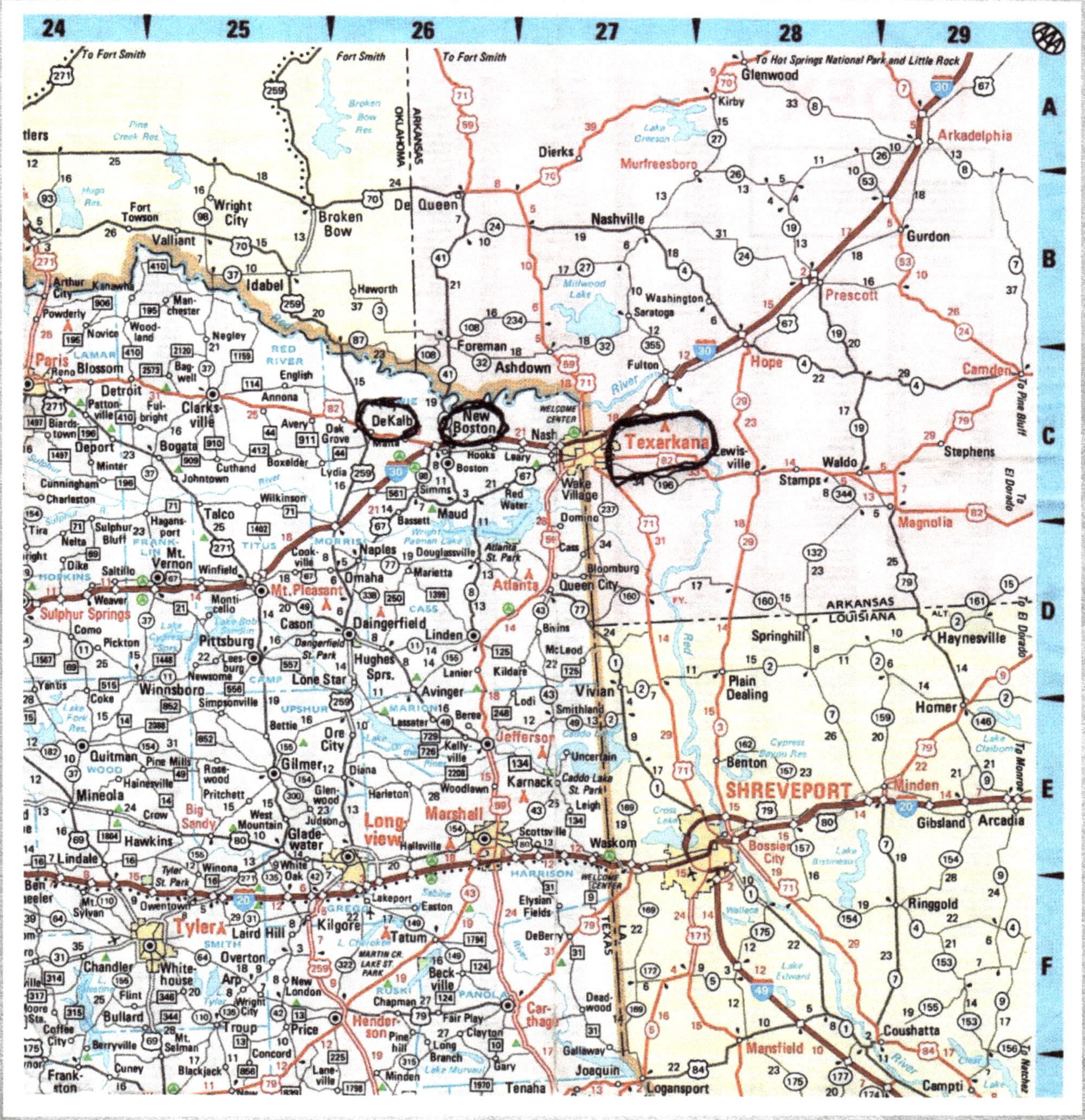

Map of Tennessee

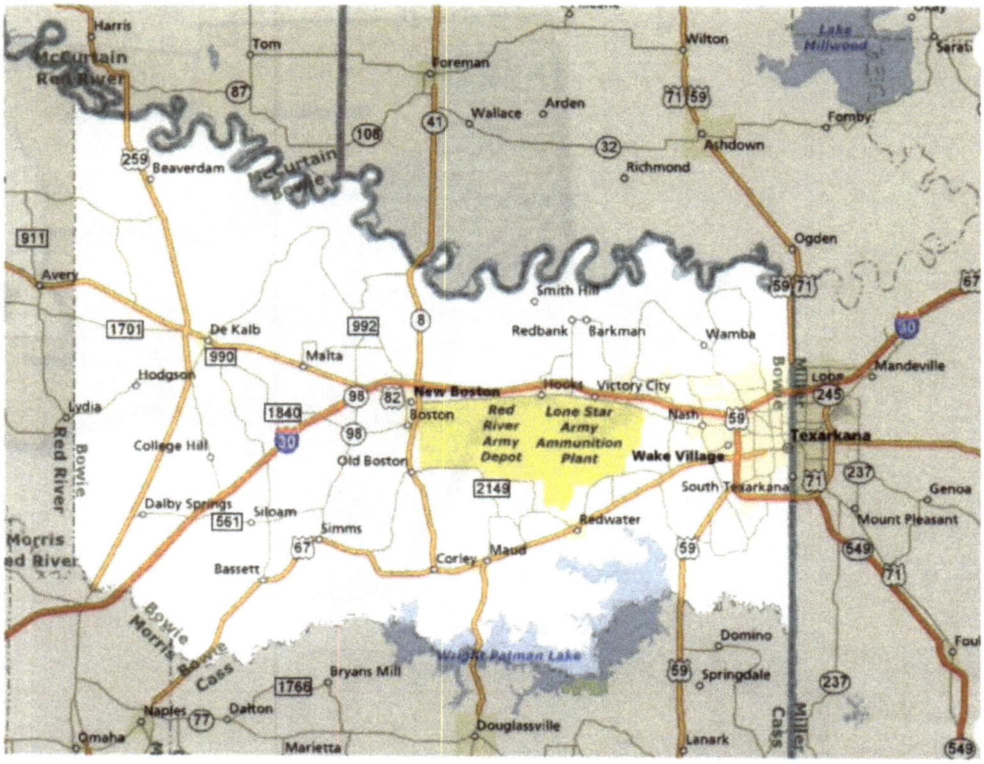

Map of Tennessee

Map of Madison County

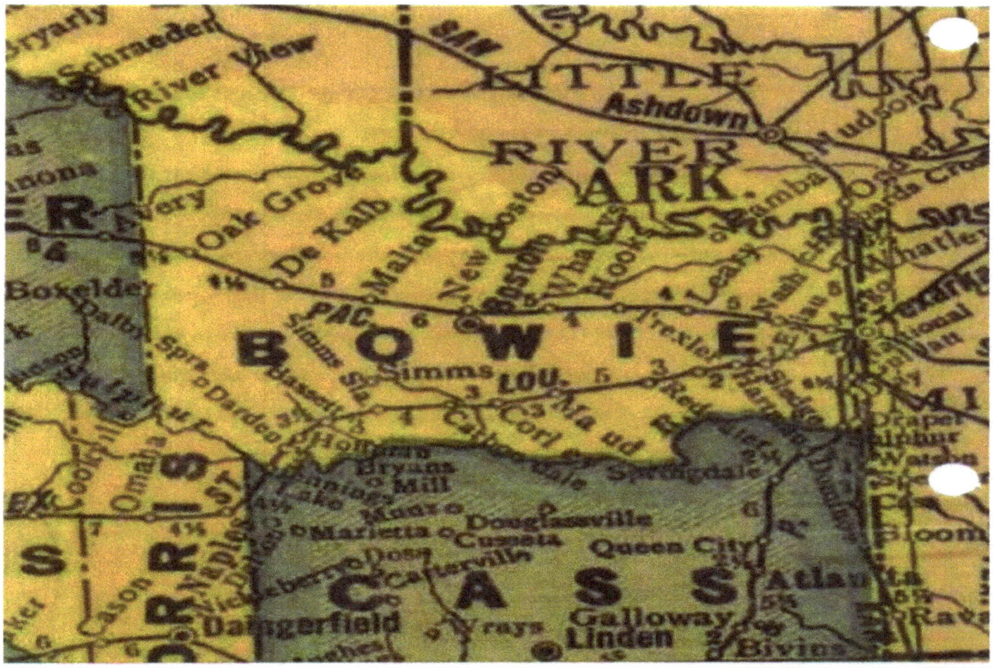

Map of Madison County

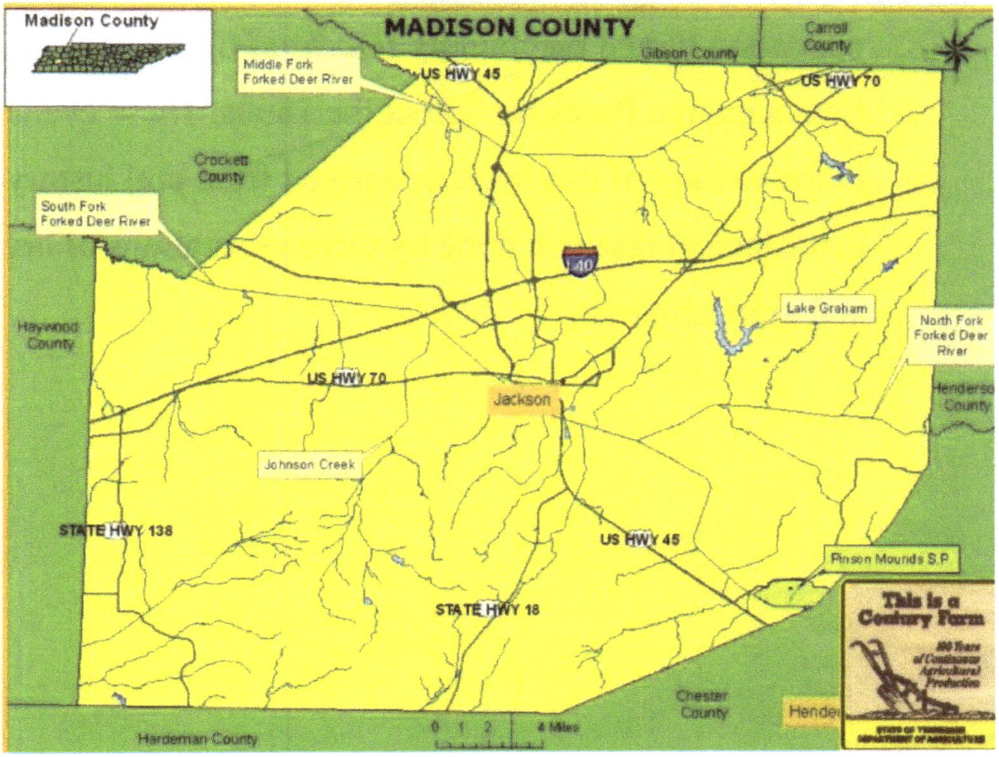

JOURNEY CONTINUED WITH RUTH GARLAND

Ruth was an Indian maiden, the mulatta daughter of Col. John C. Garland and an Indian woman. She arrived in Texas sometime between 1848 and 1858 when Col. Garland brought his family including his wife, Nancy, their children, and his slaves from Madison County, Tennessee. It was a long and tedious journey traveling by covered wagon, horseback, or walking along the way to the Mississippi River, crossing other rivers and tributaries to reach Red River and into Red River Valley to Dekalb, Texas. John Garland was moving west to find more fertile land to set up his own plantation; he also had relatives who had already moved west some years earlier.

The caravan crossed many muddy streams and valleys before reaching the county of Bowie (pr. *Boo wee*) 20 to 30 miles west of Texarkana, Texas and farther west to what he thought was *black land. Black land* was very fertile land that would yield vigorous and abundant crops of cotton. He did not reach black land because he discovered the land was not available or that it was farther west or it had been sold before he arrived. Consequently, he had to settle 12 miles inland from Red River where the soil is sandier and less likely to grow or yield large crops of cotton.

Ruth Garland (Ruthie) was the child of an Indian maiden. Her mother was born in Mississippi and she married James Garland at an early age. There were thirteen children born to them. He had been married before, but the names of his children are not known, except one (his name was Jack Garland). Our great grandmother became the wife of James Garland in about 1832. At the time "the stars fell" our grandmother was confined due to pregnancy (she was in labor) and did not see the stars fall. Grandfather was about 20 years older than our great grandmother, Ruthie. He died when he was about 90 years old.

Below is an excerpt about John Calhoun's family obtained from an unknown source at the archives of Red River County, Clarksville, Texas:

JOHN CALHOUN GARLAND AND NANCY (JOHNSON) GARLAND

John Calhoun (1810-) and Nancy (Johnson) Garland (1851-1881), born in TN, came to TX (down the Mississippi and up Red River) to near DeKalb in the late 1850's with son, Joseph Ramey Daniel (1840-1914), and a daughter, Margaret (Garland) Winston, and Mr. Winston and their daughter Lillian. An older daughter, Mary (Ms. Jimmy Sloan), had preceded them to Texas and settled at Walker Station. In 1861, John and Joe joined the Confederate army. Joe was a sergeant major in the 34th TX Calvary.

In 1867 the family bought the Wagley family house built in 1842 and land where Joe settled. His father built a house a few miles away at the Garland settlement.

On Oct. 24, 1873, Joe D. married Susan Jessie Latimer, daughter of Henry Russell and Lucinda (Shelton) Latimer of Clarksville. The Latimer family came to TX in 1833 and settled near Clarksville.

Children: (1) John "Jack" (1874-1914) operated a grocery store in Annona. (2) Nancy Lucinda (1876) m. John C. Barton (-1926), a pharmacist with a drug store on the north side of Clarksville square. (3) Jo Ella (1878-1946). (4) Leda (1880-1967). (5) Wirt Robert (1881-1968) lived in the family home his whole lifetime.

Wirt Garland graduated from Clarksville High School and attended the Univ. of TX. In 1903 he married Lola Prudence Dellinger (1881-1969), daughter of Charles Franklin and Sarah Ann Elizabeth (Eaker) Dellinger. He served in the TX Legislature and was the author of the "Farm to Marker" road bill.

Children: (1) Mary Elizabeth (Mrs. Wallace D. Armstrong). (2) Joseph Dellinger (deceased), wife, Julia (Haney) Garland. (4) Lillian Inez (Mrs. Wm. E. Nowlin).

The family home burned July 17, 1969, but the one-room log cabin the original home of the Wagley family stills stands.

Walker Station was changed to Annona in the late 1800's, named by Mr. Bill Lawson who was a Latin scholar. Annona was the Roman goddess of harvests. I had this information from Mr. Lawson himself. Joe D. Garland went to war with Lee, his body servant and friend. Once Lee was sent home for new shoes, then Jo was captured in LA. When the battle was over, Lee could not find "Marse Joe" so he went home. Joe D. spent the rest of the war in prison.

Joe D. Garland was a gay young man, liking to dance and have a good time. But after his marriage, he settled down and became an ardent churchgoer. He helped establish the first Methodist Church of Annona. As a small girl I went with him to "dinner-on-the-ground" at some of the community churches. When he died in 1914, many people came to his funeral including descendants of the black people who had come with the family from TN. The Garland Cemetery was originally a private burial ground but was finally deeded to the Methodist Church by Wirt and Roy Garland.

Joe D. Garland disapproved of baseball, which Wirt enjoyed. Wirt made the TX

University team and took care that his father should not know. Alas the team played a game that was reported in a newspaper naming Wirt was a player. Grandfather telegraphed father to return home immediately and thus ended his college and baseball career! However, he loved sports and played baseball on the Annona team in the early 1990's and tennis until his middle years.

By Mrs. W.D. Armstrong

More About Some of Ruth's Children

Jane Garland Waller

Jane Garland, my grandfather's sister, came by our home often to visit Mama. She never stayed very long. It was as though she was passing by on her way to her home. I remember once when she was passing through, by the time she arrived she had run out of snuff brushes. She would ask Millie and me to go and find a black gum bush and break off the new born branch so that she could crush the end to make a brush to dip her snuff. We would gladly do her bidding because she always had a goodie for us and would talk to us about what we would be when we grew up. We thought she was a fortune teller and could see the future. She told me that I would be a traveler and would travel far and wide.

Sarah Garland

Aunt Sarah, another sister of James Polk, lived in a small hut behind Cousin Jessie's house. When I was growing up, we thought she was like a hermit. We very seldom saw her. She never came by and we often wondered why she had the kind of isolated lifestyle that we witnessed.

Robert Garland

Robert Garland was an educator who had learned to read and write at his mother's knee. He had no formal education but knew more about education than his other sisters and brothers and was one of the first teachers in Garland Community. His picture hangs in the corridor of the school. I saw it each day as I entered the door and felt proud that he was a relative who had helped to establish a learning environment other than at home and church. He is deemed to be a great pioneer in education at Garland. Others followed including a Mr. Winston who was white: another I remember was Professor Major Johnson who taught my mother, and was known as "Professor".

Chapter 2

ON THE SEARCH

One hot summer day in July 2006 my son, Charles W., my sister, Myrtle and I stopped in Jackson, Tennessee (Madison County) at the Courthouse in route to Texas. There we found information about the Garlands who were there (Jackson, TN) before they migrated to Texas. It may have been normal to see more black people working in and around the Courthouse but to me it was unusual. Perhaps it was because Lane College is a predominantly black college founded around 1882 or after the Civil War. We were told more information could be found at the public library. We promised ourselves to return.

GARLAND CEMETERY
THE STATE OF TEXAS
BOWIE COUNTY
TEXAS
HISTORICAL
COMMISSION

DUTIES OF THE HOME

The 19th century was a time when the air was clear and unpolluted, ice cream could safely be made from fallen snow. When the sky was so bright it appeared that the moon and stars were just above your head and you should be able to reach out and touch them. During the setting of the sun, a great yellow ball sat upon the earth and you could watch it roll slowly into the ground. This was also true if one was standing beside a lake and the sun slowly sat upon the waters. Families could drink water from the springs found in open fields. During the day you could hear a neighbor calling from a mile away to his family to bring him a bucket of water and instructions for the evening meal. What he wanted for dessert, a cake or a pie or anything sweet. During this time most matrons of the homes worked in the fields only an hour or two in the morning. She then went back to the home, prepared the midday meal and returned to feed the family or field workers. She then returned to the home, prepared the supper and if need be washed the clothes and attended other duties. If there were small children, she took them with her or left them playing under a tree until she returned. If she worked while away from home, chopping cotton, hoeing planted corn, or picking cotton in the fall, the children played under the wagon. Because there were no trees in the middle of the field, shade trees kept the crops from growing.

Before children were old enough to work in the fields, my sister (Millie) and I played under the tree house. There was plenty of beautiful sand to build our castles with our feet. One could have a castle of three or more stories by using a little water. We could build a whole city though we had never seen a city.

Guineas were very poplar during my generation. Many people had them in the community. They were used mainly as guard dogs. Whenever a stranger entered the premises they would sing a loud warning song different from everyday singing and you would look out the window to see who was around. This was common because there were not many visitors. Occasionally a vendor would come by selling apples or other fruit, but we were careful about who we bought from. I can remember vendors coming by in their wagons. My mother was not very pleased because they would address her as "auntie," a salutation abhorred by my mother because it implied familiarity that she did not invite and she tried to insult them by answering, "I'm not your aunt." They did the same with my father by calling him "uncle." They finally learned better because they were insulted. Most times they were as poor as we were.

OUR HOUSE

This is the house where the author and her siblings grew up. It was built in 1929 during the depression, and because of short funds, was not completely finished at the time of construction. When it was first built, only the areas necessary for living were finished and even they were slow to be completed. All of the rooms were eventually finished by about 1935. The old house (the first house my mama and daddy had) located on what we called the "Old Place," was torn down and some of the lumber was carried to the new place to help build this house in the drawing. Millie and I played on the stack of lumber from the old house that had been piled there quite a while. We made up songs and danced and sang about Lawrence Thorne, our Aunt Zilpha's brother. Lawrence Thorne was a sporty man, with keep features. A tall, well dressed fellow, he stopped by and visited us from time to time. Aunt Zippha (pronounced Zil-fee) was Uncle Jim Garland's wife. Uncle Jim was my mother's brother. Lawrence Thorne would sometimes tell us stories and bring us little "tidbits." We loved him and thought he was the greatest man around, except for our brothers and father. He was the uncle of our playmates, Agnes and Earline and little Lawrence Thorne who live on the hill (Red Clay Hill). We visited our playmates many Sunday evenings.

Names	Age	Wed	Spouse	Age
Jim Polk-Garland	1850-1923	1872	Jennie Knight	1858-1888
I. Jossie Garland	1874-1893		I. William Shavers, Sr.	1868-1965
A. Ethel Shavers	18__-1918		A. Clayton Bell	18__-1970
1. Eloise Bell	1914		1. C. Barrett	
2. Iverson Bell	1917		2. Ethel Davis	
II. Mollie Garland	Baby			
III. Effie Garland	1876-19__		III. William Shavers, Sr.	1867-1965
IV. Jim Garland	1878-1957		IV. Zilphia Thornes	1886-19
V. Hart Garland	1880-1913		V. Lititia Estes	
A. Zether Garland	1802-19		A. Cornelius Webb	
1. Loys Webb	- 19		1.Nancy	
a. Alaistair Webb				
VI. Smithie Garland	1882-19		VI. John Hubbard, St.	18__-1936
VII. Charlie Garland	Baby			
VIII. Laura Garland	1886-1983		VIII. Robert Shavers	18__-1959
2nd Wife – no children				
Jim Polk Garland	Same	1896	Millie Walker	18__-19__

SHELTER

Taking shelter is critical in times of disaster. Shelter is appropriate when conditions require that you seek protection in your home, place of employment, or other location where you are when disaster strikes. Sheltering outside the hazard area would include staying with friends and relatives, seeking commercial lodging, or staying in a mass care facility operated by disaster relief groups in conjunction with local authorities.

To effectively shelter, you must first consider the hazard and then choose a place in your home or other building that is safe for that hazard. For example, for a tornado, a room should be selected that is in a basement or an interior room on the lowest level away from corners, windows, doors and outside walls. Because the safest locations to seek shelter vary by hazard, sheltering is discussed in the various hazard sections. These discussion include recommendations for sealing the shelter if the hazard warrants this type of protection.

Even though mass care shelters often provide water, food, medicine, and basic sanitary facilities, you should plan to take your disaster supplies kit with you so you will have the supplies you require. Mass care sheltering can involve living with many people in a confined space, which can be difficult and unpleasant. To avoid conflicts in this stressful situation, it is important to cooperate with shelter managers and others assisting them. Keep in mind that alcohol beverages and weapons are forbidden in emergency shelters and smoking is restricted.

The length of time you are required to shelter may be short, such as during a tornado warning, or long, such as during a winter storm. It is important that you stay in a shelter until local authorities say it is safe to leave. Additionally, you should take turns listening to radio broadcasts and maintain a 24-hour safety watch.

During extended periods of sheltering, you will need to manage water and food supplies to ensure you and your family have the required supplies and quantities.

- Guidelines for managing water supplies
- Guidelines for managing food supplies

Both grandparents had storm shelters. Families gathered to take cover when storms were approaching.

FEMA: SHELTER
SURVIVAL KIT

<u>THINGS YOU NEED TO KNOW TO SURVIVE ON A FARM</u>

1. Learn to walk a log before bridges are washed away
2. Learn to wring a chicken's neck, to pluck chicken feathers, to make pillows or a mattress from the feathers,
   and how to dress the chicken for a meal
3. Learn to drive a team and wagon, make a slide, drive a horse or mule or tractor
4. Learn how to milk a cow
5. If cattle become ill with a serious disease, learn how to slaughter and bury them and start another herd.
6. Learn how to build a storm house under ground
7. Expect the best, be prepared for the worse

8. Keep your eyes open for vermin
9. Learn the rules of cleanliness
10. Learn how to cook and serve a meal
11. Learn how to split wood to make shingles to cover the roof
12. Learn how to make lye soap
13. Learn how to repair a barbed wire fence
14. Learn how to find water with a stick and how to dig a well
15. Learn how to build a flue
16. Learn how to read the clouds for an approaching storm
17. Learn how to fish and where to dig for bait and know the kinds of fish in rivers and streams around you
18. Learn what to do in the case of a fire or storm
19. Learn who to call in case of illness or birth of a child
20. Learn how to cook outside and how to start a fire in the wilderness
21. Learn how to wash clothes without a washing machine
22. Learn how to handle a plow
23. Learn how to make a mound to plant a watermelon seed and later to till when the watermelon is ripe...if all else fails, ask your mother or father
24. Learn the social graces, how to sing and dance
25. Learn how to kill a snake; know the snakes in your neighborhood
26. Learn to shoot a gun
27. Learn the skill of farming
28. Learn that a wise man carries a coat
29. Learn the environment, plants that are edible and those that are not
30. Learn the names of trees, flowers, their leaves and their bark structure at a glance
31. Greet all strangers eye to eye
32. Seek out your Higher Power
33. "Walk softly, but carry a big stick"
34. Save money and goods for hard times
35. Give or share with others the best you have
36. Learn the "Golden Rule"
37. Learn the Ten Commandments
38. Count your blessings
39. Have the faith and pray

ARTIFACTS

Petrified wood has been found on the farm from prehistoric times. Dinosaur bones and other artifacts have been found in caves less than 12 miles away near Red River Bank by a cousin, C. Ellis who demonstrated his find in DeKalb Public Schools many times.

Four States Fair Will Exhibit Bones of Prehistoric Monster

Some of the dinosaur bones found north of New Boston and classified by a museum curator as the bones of a prehistoric monster that roamed in this area 25,000,000 to 50,000,000 years ago will be exhibited at the Four States Fair, W. N. Harkness, local attorney, said Wednesday.

The bones were located on an old gravel bed near Spanish Bluff on the Red river on land owned by Hargett Ellis, a Negro farmer, who made the discovery.

Ellis found the unusually large and heavy bones many years ago, but the classification was not made until recently when Harkness became interested.

Harkness was running a survey line in the area in preparation for a court case when Ellis showed him some bones and teeth he had found.

He had some additional bones and teeth in a corn crib at his home. They were gleanings of several years.

Harkness borrowed three of the larger pieces and sent them to Strecker Museum at Baylor University for classification. The classification was made by Professor Bryce C. Brown, assistant curator of the museum who came here to further study the find and submit a preliminary report to the university.

He gathered a few fragments himself for further study, and said the bones and teeth he examined came from a dinosaur that roamed in the lower or upper Cretaceous era.

Professor Brown said the structure of the teeth showed that the dinosaur was a herbivorous type (plant eating), but could not fix the species of monster until he had studied it further.

There are about 12 known general types of dinosaurs and at least several of these are known to have ranged in the western world not covered by water in the Cretaceous era.

These monster ranged from seven feet in length and up to 50 tons in weight.

Professor Brown said the skull and teeth are the best identification.

He said that on the basis of his survey he was satisfied that the river was washing the bones from the actual deposit in which the dinosaur died. "The real site must have been quicksand, a tar pit, or similar deposit. The dinosaur was trapped and died in this formation," he said.

Professor Brown said the actual deposit might be a "gold mine" of tremendous value to researchers.

Professor Brown said the vertebrae found are larger than the span of two hands. He said the find also includes the bones of one or two other animals, possibly a mammoth, an elephant-like creature.

He said that the fact that the bones are heavy indicate that they are fossils as bones gain weight with great age. "When you compare a bone of an early age with even a large bone, say of an elephant of this age, the fossil is much heavier because of the chemical changes it has undergone," he explained.

The Texas-born professor left here for the University of Michigan to complete studies for a doctor's degree.

He will have the staff at the university further check the find he collected. He is seeking to borrow the teeth for study, but Ellis has thus far declined to release them.

Archeologists Study Sites In Texarkana

Members of the State and Southern Methodist University Archeological Societies were in Texarkana Thursday and Friday to tour the many historic and prehistoric sites in the area.

Curtis Tunnell, State Archeologist, State Building Commission, R. K. Harris, Research Archeologist for Southern Methodist University and Jay Blaine, Director, Texas Archeological Society, viewed collections of artifacts from this area Thursday at the Chamber of Commerce.

The Texarkana area is rich in prehistoric Indian sites which cover a time span of six to eight thousand years. Unfortunately, these sites are rapidly disappearing because of urban expansion, construction, and from the many people digging who know nothing of archeological excavation or who don't seem to care for the historical value of the sites.

In a few years much of the rich prehistoric heritage of this area will be gone unless steps are taken immediately to preserve a few of the Indian mounds and campsites.

The Texarkana area is also rich in historic sites. One of the most significant marks in Northeast Texas is the site of the French fort and trading post, Fort Saint Louis, built on Red River by LaHarpe in 1719. This site along with another on Red River was visited by the group Thursday afternoon.

Tunnell said he greatly appreciated the land owners of the area who permitted the group to tour sites that were on their land.

1966

TEXARKANA GAZETTE, TEXARKANA,

One day during the latter of August in the 1960s when we (Mattie, Charles and children) went home to DeKalb, my mother and I were talking about the earlier days when we worked in the field and how early we had to leave in the morning to make breakfast. I said to her, "Oh yes mama, there's an old ax out in the wood pile, may I have it? It is old, does not have a handle, and is rusting in the ground." "Sure, she said, take anything you want."

The picture of the old ax blade is one my father chopped wood with to make a fire for heating and especially cooking breakfast. I keep it in the drawer to remind me of my humble beginnings.

After the rooster crowed one could hear the sound of the blade against the wood miles away and a "hacking" reply with the echo.

Smoking was not a good idea but my father smoked a pipe and cigars. I also kept one of his pipes, one that I sent him on his birthday. He died November 17, 1959 at the age of 87 years old.

Quilts for the Children

There were never enough quilts to cover the children during winter and my mother wanted her children to stay warm. We never had heat at night though hot coals were kept alive to start a fire in the morning. Consequently my mother stitched scraps of material together large enough to make a quilt. She lined the center with a layer of cotton and lined that with "broadcloth" or some other durable material and placed the quilt on long rollers placed on "horses" and quilted the quilt in a pattern she desired. Later years when she wanted her children to have a "keepsake," she collected nylon stockings, bleached them and died them again and made each child a quilt. I still have not quilted mine but the oldest children's quilts were quilted before she died.

Chapter 3

SHORT STORIES AND MEMORIES

Voices from the Past

In the recesses of my mind I can still hear Mother Laura Garland Shavers, talking, half to herself and half to me as we walked the periphery of the farm to bring food for the noon meal to other workers in the field. Hand on hip she would say "we need to clean this section and that section of trees to grow better crops." She would continue and say: "We need to find shelter for this or that tool, rather than leave it in the field to rust and decay." She would continue with many other "we need to's." I can hear the voice of my Uncle Jim Garland who had a farm adjacent to my parents talking to "Old Blue" giving commands of "Ge or haw" which meant to go right or left and another neighbor to his son, Charlie, calling for him to go to the house and bring him a bucket of water to cool his head and throat. He was about one-fourth of a mile away plowing the cane fields.

The voices of our preachers or minister, Reverend Sexton and the principle, Professor U. S. McClellan still ring in my ears.

We were approximately four years old and traveled alone. My first trip away from home with Millie, my twin, was a trip to Hooks, Texas, 25 miles away plus about ten miles to Aunt Smithey's on the T&P train that comes through DeKalb from Fort Worth. We were dressed in beautiful velvet black and red smocked yoke dresses, patent leather shoes and tan finely woven socks that looked like silk and up to our knees. Our sister, Laura Pearl had made these beautiful dresses. She made all our clothes. She was, as I remember a very fine seamstress, a very hard worker who supported the family in every way with every fiber of her being. She had many talents and used each one with the tenacity of a wild animal.

I am sure the trip took no longer than an hour (the trains were slow) but to me it was a life time adventure, an exposure to the outside world.

It is alleged that Cousin Emma, Jessie Garland's wife was a "live wire." She once said, "I will cut thorns till I see no bush."

Mail Boxes on a Buggy Wheel

All mail was delivered on the main road. If one lived on the back of the community, he/she had to walk all the way (or ride) to the front road to receive mail. The boxes were mounted and names on the spokes of a buggy wheel. (Turn the wheel to your box). (Good trip for the day).

Healing Waters

During the late 1800s and latter part of this century, it was alleged that Dolby Springs, (a small town near DeKalb), was a health resort that boasted of healing waters. Many of the families living in Garland came from Dolby Springs, namely the McGowns, the Hunters, the Walkers, Mobleys and Stevens.

The railroad ran to DeKalb from this town after slavery just this year 2007 a lady living in a rest home from Dolby Springs in DeKalb, passed (died); she was 115 years old.

She must have taken advantage of the healing water of Dolby Springs.

Short Story

Around the giant pin oak tree are artifacts of Indian arrows.
They remind me of the earth sands artfully placed among grass heaps and time gone by when hunters stalked their kill, armed with decision at will.

See the color dancing by with feathers perched on high,
Hear the chanting and dancing feet as they tip toe swiftly nearby

Stop and pick your favorite rock flint
Sharpened to flint-cut the foe
Swift as the sunlight passes through as the breeze shadows creep by as tall as the trees memories pass by and return to tease

There were white sand-beds on the farm littered with flint rock arrow heads left by the Indian hunters at the back of the farm called "The Old Place" where the family farmed around a large pin oak tree. There were so many broken rocks at times, it was hard to find enough soil for cotton or corn or workers to tend the growth for the plants on this plot of land.

Before "Dehornment"

Texas was and is still known for its large cattle ranching industry. The cattle were shipped in large numbers to Kansas City where the beef was packaged and distributed throughout the nation. Many southern black men after slavery migrated to Kansas to work in the meat packing houses. When I was a child, I would watch these cattle with their long horns being herded from the west towards Kansas City. The Cows were often fighting one another using their horns. I suppose it eventually became practical to dehorn the animals before herding them to their destination. However, I remember how long before "dehornment," it was a frightening sight to a small child to see cattle being driven from the west and through the Garland Community close by on highway 82 to Texarkana to board a train for Kansas City. If the herd was too large, they might be herded all the way to Kansas City. One could hear and sometimes see the cowboys popping their whips and talking cowboy hearding language which sounded like "he' ah he'ah" in a high pitch. The cattle were lowing in pain or resentment, a sight to see and hear, seldom seen even today on television.

It seemed a necessary evil because the people needed, or they thought they needed, beef to survive. Never a necessary evil because the people needed, or they thought they needed beef to survive. Nevertheless, I still hear the "lowing" of the herd, and see the cowboys in their "ten gallon" hats, their chaps blowing in the wind, the clicking of the spurs, the colors of their vests, and most of all the whistles of the cowboys as they say western songs after sundown. (In my mind's ear) one could hear clicking of spurs against the stirrups and hear bodies rubbing against leather chaps.

Stories

When I graced the earth, *Jim Crow* was alive and well. African Americans were still considered "less than" free citizens. "Less than," two words meaning not equal to our white counterparts. Poor whites, blacks and people of mixed races were all treated inhumanely. Blacks could not use public facilities if marked or labeled white only; they could not drink from the same fountains or ride on buses or on trains, except in the back. They were excluded from many places which were labeled for whites only. Blacks did not worship in the same churches or buy a car or land unless signed for or sanctioned by a white person. Men could not wear hats in the presence of whites. Jobs were only service jobs such as cleaning, cooking, ironing, working in the fields or jobs the white person did not do. They could not vote until voter rights became legal, and even then a questionnaire was required that was so difficult that only persons who had earned a Ph.D. could answer it. They could not walk on the street unless they moved nearly off the street when passing a white. If one raised a crop and took it to market, the white man took your money and told you that you didn't need it. If you complained, you were slammed in jail. You had to always enter the back door, and you were always addressed by your first name. It was a miserable life, but black people were strong and survived the insults, lynchings, rapes of women, and other unspeakable acts.

The Cat Hole

A creek ran through the community of Garland. My father told us it was called "Lon Creek." A great portion of that creek ran through my grandfather's farm on the land that my mother inherited. There was a bend in the creek we called the "cat hole." This hole was very deep and never ran dry. One could almost always catch a few fish for supper there if you could get permission from your parents to go fishing. You could never go alone. Millie and I were always fortunate to have our older brother by two and half years, Iverson (Honey), with us during the early days of spring. He could swim and hunt, in addition to having other skills to protect us. I can still feel the cool breeze, hear the birds singing, the wind blowing softly, the cork going under and retrieving a beautiful catfish. We dug our own worms from under the sweet gum tree near the farm where they were always plentiful.

Man of Hope

Down the dusty white and occasionally red clay road to one and a half miles west of DeKalb, Texas, the old horse drawn buggy pulled onto Jim Garland Lane (not so named at that time) to a gate on the right. He alighted the small carriage to open the gate made of bobbed wire stretched in between a wooden post on each end. He stepped back upon the buggy and rode over to the house, past the china berry tree to the barn. I had rushed home to feed the stock before sundown. Guineas had begun their announcement of the coming event of the sinking golden ball surrounded by incoming grey and fading blue. My grandfather, James P. Garland, was a farmer, a businessman, and a tenant owner who had servants, a large amount of acreage, horses, cows, goats, pigs, chickens, and guineas. He was a community activist and trustee of the Garland school.

When he approached the barn, he discovered that "Ole' Bell," the lead cow, was missing. She always had her bell and yoke around her neck, but this time the bell was missing and Grandpa had to look for her. When he got to the house, it was dark. Grandma Millie asked, "What happened?" He said, "Bell was missing, I had to find her. I found her under a tree just chewing her cud. I guess she got tired and had to rest. She is getting old you know." "Come on in," she said, "supper is on the table."

Baptism

My sister and I were baptized in the old swimming pool. It was just a hole in the ground, an indenture left by the flood of the creek. We were wrapped in white sheets for the ceremony. The preacher, in his white robe, was standing up to his waist in the water with his assistant. I was shaking all over. I had never learned to swim and did not know how to hold my breath. My turn came next; the preacher said, while he held his hand over my nose and held my waist and shoulders, "I baptize you in the name of the Father, Son, and the Holy Ghost," and submerged me. I got so strangled that I thought I would die before I could climb the banks of the pool. My mother was waiting with a towel, but all my brothers and sisters were looking and I cried.

Fishing With Our Father

We spent the night on the warm banks of "Anderson Creek." Most of the afternoon was spent fishing for anything that dared to "sink our corks." When the sun disappeared and sank below the edge of the earth, we made our pallets upon the leaves, topping them with soft quilts. With our heads on pillows, we were covered with small fleecy blankets and the sky above. We dreamed and reminisced with the moon until our eyelids closed to the singing and falsetto of the night. Dawn came soon, and again all creeping, crawling, and flying creatures joined their voices of praise to awaken us. We had dressed our catch the evening before and now it was time to break the fast. After a wash up and with a fire of twigs, a skillet, and hot grease, we silenced the hunger from yesterday. Next came more fishing as we retrieved another catch. It was time then to withdraw our lines and pack our tackle for home. We had been on a journey for bonding with enough joy to fill our hearts flowing with love until the next time.

Play House

Down the lane under the spreading pen oak tree we played house. There was plenty of water in a very low branch that never ran dry. There was also plenty of dirt to pretend we were cooking. We could mix the soil and water to make pretend food. We made meat, bread, and vegetables or any shape we wanted, placing these shapes in the sun to dry. After drying we would place them on a make-believe plate and pretend to eat. This exercise could last many hours until mama called us in.

The Sweet Gum Tree

(Genus: Liquidamber)

The sweet gum tree has taken its place in the annals of trees as a lovely subject. Its uses are very few, but in the fall of the year, its leaves rival the best of all trees in beauty: red, yellow and gold. But for me, the sap from this tree was a mighty fine chew. Down the lane during fall, if a cut had been made in the tree trunk, its precious fluid flowed like white wine and became solid. It was the chew of the day for many children looking for something to chew. We chewed it until our jaws became numb, and after the chew we took it out and plastered it under the table to be chewed again by anyone. Sweet gum trees litter the farm where I grew up. Each spring they had to be chopped down. They grew so fast between fall and spring that farmers had to clear the ground of them before preparing to put in a new crop of corn and cotton for the new-year.

Dancing, Singing, Dress Code and Other Practices

Before my birth and during my early years, dancing in public was not permitted. Only marching single file was allowed. We would march in from the playground after school recess. Back into the school we'd march with music playing and students stepping in time with the rhythm.

Most of the songs for public singing were spiritual or religious songs. Even for adults, non-classical or non-religious music was considered immoral. One would not even be caught patting one's foot to blues or jazz tunes for example. Unacceptable music like this was referred to as "the reels." There was one classical ballad that my husband's grandmother, Susana McDaniel, had had ground into her system so deeply that she always found herself tapping her foot. When one day she heard Charles playing a recording of it, she asked, "Charles is them the 'reels?" He said, "No," so she continued to pat her foot enthusiastically, re-assured that the music was socially condoned.

Dancing was a no, no, and certainly no touching was allowed. The "dress code" was also very strict. No bearing of flesh, legs or arms in public. Courting was done while riding in the buggy or wagon with a chaperone, and one had to always be home before dark, young or old. Men wore their "Sunday best" with a "cravath" and a long gold chain that had a round gold watch hanging from a watch pocket. Women never cut their hair; if they did, they were called "floosies," and they always wore long dresses or shirts down to their high top shoes or boots.

On The Farm

Farm Animals

There were many farm animals on the farm. Mom and Dad were not considered to be ranchers but the chores involved were similar. During my life on the farm, at the times there were approximately 20-30 and sometimes more cows (20-30), six or more horses, eight to ten pigs and goats each plus many chickens, geese used to keep the grass down in the field and occasionally, to be plucked, to stuff pillows or mattresses. The horses and the adult cows had names and sometimes the chickens. It took all of us to do the chores. Each person had the responsibility of caring for something, and we accompanied Honey (our brother) when he had to look for the cows when they did not come home on their own.

We often had to wade across the creek just before sun down with Lee our dog at our side guiding the cows' home. We mended fences (this was for men). House duties were for the women. Sometimes women had to milk the cows, a chore I learned well but hated to do. I loved gardening of vegetables and flowers as I continue to love even today. When chores were slow for children we were allowed to go fishing. There were plenty of pools and creeks for that when the weather permitted or the season was right. Many times we were allowed to go alone and many times our father accompanied us. He enjoyed fishing and hunting. I never learned to hunt but my brothers especially Honey was a marksman. He was also our protector. Mommy and Dad trusted him to be with us at all times.

By the time I arrived on the scene, the Children of Ruth had practice the same lifestyle since slavery. Many of them had good homes but many of the amenities had not or were not available to the inhabitants of Garland Community. There was no electricity for lighting or cooking. But many years before there had been a form of communications. The telephone post was still there. But for some reason the wires were not activated and were not so until the 1940s--- certainly for some after World War II.

After World War II, improvements were made in every spectrum. The Depression came during the late 1920s which brought changes. One can never imagine but many of Ruth's Children lost their homes, their small bank savings were depleted and were told by bankers they didn't have need for it – all the savings were stolen and no job available. There were people on soup lines and begging. We burned coal oil for lamps and heating.

Short Story

I haven't heard of one of the members of the "Clan" killing another person, but I have heard of a few "eye-balling" one or the other sex being shot at, or being hit in the finger because of an unnamed woman just before he ducked behind a tree or was threatened with a 44 or 32 because of improper behavior becoming a gentleman. But as far as I can tell they obeyed the golden rule. "Thou shalt not covenant thy neighbor's wife or anything that is thy neighbor," just before he ducked behind a tree a few exceptions. These are a few exceptions taking a few ears of corn for breakfast.

I have heard about a gentleman raiding the corn field or watermelon patch or stealing the peaches off the trees, or picking fresh black-eyed peas or dry peas from the patch; hiding cattle in the cane thicket from being counted by officials, or picking up a gallon of syrup made from freshly ground cane from the mill.

Noon Bell

One could tell the time of day by the saw mill whistle, morning, noon and evening, because the whistle could blow out loud and clear, heard all over the community. This was very helpful because around 11:00 o'clock in the morning when the sun bore down on the backs in the field of workers it was music to the ears because they knew that noon was soon to come. If mamma did not bring lunch to us; we walked about three quarters of a mile or a mile home to get it. The farm ran about that distance through the woods and across the creek. Even so, it was very relaxing to get an hour away from the fields and job at hand. We took a 30 minute nap after lunch before returning to the field.

Fall To Winter, Interlude

In the late fall, October or November, was a time to store food for winter. I was fortunate to join in the preparation of potatoes (sweet and white) shucking corn for chickens and animals, shucking peanuts, gathering wild fruit (grapes, blue berries, musquidines) peeling walnuts – a system of using a board with a small hole in it – gathering hickory nuts or pecans.

Gathering pecans was always fun. Burying and banking vegetables was also fun. We didn't have many pecan trees so if we wanted to have them; we had to go to near Red River with Cousin Harry (Ulysses) to pick them up on what we called "halves"; half to us and half to Aunt Smithy in Hooks, TX. We often went by wagon but if any family member had a T-model Ford, we could ask if they would drive us to the site.

Once our father took us by wagon to Aunt Effie --- we could keep all the berries we could find; and once we were taken by our brother Fred near Red River --- there he taught school, in the old T-model Ford. All these trips were great fun and plenty of nuts to eat during the winter.

Winter Needs

Also during late fall men in the family saved wood, mainly the dry or fallen trees and saved the split wood in chords for winter to be used for heating and cooking. We used the pot-bellied stove for heating. The fire place was never complete, but we generally had a fancy stove for cooking with big, warming bin (cooking oven or other features). There were always plenty quilts, pillows made by downs from geese, feather pillows and handmade bed covers.

Just after winter and about a month before spring was the hardest time of the year; food had been used up and very little if any money left. Often, floods came and wells fell-in. It meant hard work all over again.

The Bell

The bell spoke many languages, time to rest, time to eat, time to announce the dead . . .

After more than 20 years I can still hear the bell in the belfry at the old Methodist church tolling just before the cock crowed for sundown. Someone in the community had died. Was it one of my cousins, my uncle, my aunt or my friend? It had been announced in church that someone was ill. How could they perish so soon? My heart skipped a beat or two. The tolling went on for what seemed to be an hour but was only a slow and mournful few minutes. These minutes gave one time to review or reflect upon all the good or bad memories of that person. Did he/she attend church, or follow any of the "Golden Rules" as we were taught? Or was he/she just my loved one? My heart wanted to pound out of my chest and I wept…and I wept….

The Precocious One

Millie, my twin sister, was so far ahead of the rest of us in her readings and knowledge of the Bible when we were kids. When it came her time to say a short blessing before a meal, as it was the custom we as children were required to do, her blessing was from Psalm 103:2--- from the Holy Bible: "Bless the Lord God my soul and all that is within me. Bless God's Holy name. Bless the Lord, O my soul, and forget not all His benefits." That was a lot to say for a little girl. The rest of us might have said something like "God is love" so that we could hurry and eat, but she had to say all of this! How we laughed and snickered at our sister!

Water

Water on the farm is a precious commodity. Many times during the summer, the creek bed became almost dry. Without water the creeks dried up and the animals suffered. Hay was ruined.

There were no nuts or berries. If a family did not have a deep well to water the stock, the stock could die. Some community inhabitants knew how to find water or where to dig a well. They insisted that there was a technique to finding water. They swore that by finding a special kind of tree and a branch shaped in a special way, one could grab the fork or two branches of a forked limb, walk over a suspected place where water could be and determine if there was water there. If the fork rebelled from being held or quivered, one could be sure that water would be found there.

Rain Barrel

In the old house where we lived before the new house was built in 1929, the house was shaped like an upside down "L." At the precipice or angle, a rain barrel was placed on the ground. This barrel caught enough water to do at least two washings of clothes for a family of eleven and maybe enough to use in cooking for a week. The water was 'soft" and much better than well water for that purpose, and it was used whenever there was a problem with the well.

Rain Maker

Our cousin, Charles Haynes, thought he had the power to make it rain. During the hot crackling dry season (July and August) when it did not rain, he cut trees on his farm, piled the logs in a special manner, and set them a-fire. He insisted that the smoke would pollute clouds and cause the rain to come down. Sometimes this worked …or did it? He certainly would keep trying until it did rain. We would see that smoke and say "Oh! Old Charlie's gonna make it rain!"

Games Children Play

The smaller and younger children of Ruth's descendants still play: *Hide and Go Seek, Mary Mack, Here We Go Round the Mulberry Bush, Rope Jumping, Hop Scotch, See Saw, Jacks, Bubble Blowing*, and other games when children are together.

There was an atmosphere and spirit of joy in Garland when I was a child. There was also a willingness to change when change was all around in a world subjected to change through creativity, technology, and the normal and inevitable change. Each moment of each day we were mobilized by this phenomenon and moved forward each day with dreams and hope in our hearts.

Growing Up

While growing up from about four to ten years old, Millie and I spent some time with our cousin, Love Hubbard (Geneva) daughter of Smithy Garland Hubbard, my mother's sister. Aunt Smithy and her husband Uncle John lived in Hooks, Texas about 15 miles from DeKalb on a "black land farm." They were considered to be "very well off," with a beautiful home, cars, huge work horses and riding horses, cows, and large gardens with fruits of many sorts, a self-playing organ and other well-appointed furnishings such as a large radio. We were free to play and run about and play on a shallow pool in the front yard with a pet goat or chase the many turkeys around the yard and farm. They had stored in the smoke house and storage house many hams and barrels of nuts including walnuts, hickory nuts, pecans and imperishable vegetables as potatoes, onions, peas and beans and a farm filled with corn, peas, maize, etc. Needless to say, we always had a good time at Aunt Smithy's house although at time we fought and disagreed as we played; we had many stories to tell when we returned home about going to church, baptism and other episodes such as slipping off to go to the Red River banks and boarding a fishing boat.

Slipping Away

When Millie and I wanted to slip away, our excuse was, "We're going to the spring to get a pail of water." Water was always needed (especially spring water) after the well behind the house fell in. Millie loved books…*any* book. She would hide under anything to read, bed or tree. So away we went either to the playhouse under the spreading pin oak tree, which was down the lane on the way to the mail box, or to the spring for a tiny sand bar island where the willows stood.

Laura Pearl

Second oldest daughter of Laura V. Garland-Shavers was Laura Pearl Shavers Sands; named for her mother Laura and Laura's best friend in college (Bishop College), Pearl Alexander. My mother spoke often of her friend and sometimes they exchanged letters. Laura Pearl (Pearl) had many talents. She cared very deeply for us. She fed, clothed, taught, played, reprimanded, cooked, cleaned and even served my mother as a breast-pump, nursing her when she became so uncomfortable with swollen breasts. We depended on her for everything. Oh! How we loved her!

The Old Split Rail Fence

The rail fence had almost disappeared when I arrived on the scene. I remember seeing a short one when coming from my uncle's farm while riding in a wagon. He lived in a community near Red River and we (my siblings and I) went often to visit or to work during "harvest time" to help him gather his crop. Change came when barbed wire was used for fencing. In most recent years, a single wire, electrically charged, is used on some farms.

Townships

There were three (3) townships in Garland owned by Professor L. M. Johnson (a post office called Booker and store) Robert S. Shavers and Jessie Garland.

The one my father owned was supplied with most staples, (food) that a family needed to survive on mostly dried or processed food, coal oil, small tools, tobacco, candy, school supplies.

In 1929 when the Country was in depression, most people in the community had little to live on, no banks (we had only one or two) would allow us to borrow. They were "broke' too or closed. The small amount of amenities in my father's store were few.

Neighbors borrowed from my father until the store became "broke." It closed and never became active again. But while it was alive, Honey, Millie and I enjoyed an occasional "mud ball." A large chocolate ball enough for three kids, while their parents were not at home. Honey was the care taker for a brief time.

Saturday Night and Sunday Morning Baths

Saturday night or Sunday morning were times to take a good bath. Any other time was a "Cat Bath time" (wipe off). There were two no 3 tubs used for washing clothes (washing and rinsing) and bathing "our saving grace."

The old iron tea kettle was put on the stove, filled to the top to reach the boiling point. This hot water was added to about four gallons of water for the bath. Clean underwear was put out early "union ware"… to be worn for a week, clean towels for washing and drying and any kind of soap available, usually soap was to wash cloths.

The children had a mutual tub. The oldest twins went first. Then the next was the other set of twins and then the baby. We were now ready to prepare for Sunday school until the next week.

Human Interest and Short Poems

I was told Ruth's daughter, was married to a Koleium and again to a slave Garland from another branch of the Garland clan. She was a "Blood Line Garland."

Grand Pa Polk had an adopted son named Dallas. When it came time for Dallas to be baptized, he was wading in the pool to the preacher. The preacher, Reverend Koleium, was married to Aunt Jane Waller. Dallas was wading over to be baptized during this sacred ceremony. As the waters became deeper and rose up to his shoulders he yelled out in a fearful voice "Too deep Mr. Koleium" He never went into the water again.

Chapter 4

COMMUNITY OF GARLAND

It Matters but Little How Long We Live

Author unknown

It matters but little how long we live
In this world of sorrow sin and care,
Whether in youth you're taken away
Or live till your bones in your feet are bare.
But whether you do the best you can
To lighten the weight of adversities,
Touch on the fainting brow of a fellow man,
I tell you my sister and brothers
It matters much!
It matters much!

This short poem was often quoted by my mother, Laura Garland, at public gatherings in the Community of Garland.

OTHER PARTS OF THE COMMUNITY

The Church

By the time children reached twelve years old, it was expected that they would become full-fledged members of the church. There were two churches in the community, Baptist and Methodist. We became Baptist because our father was Baptist. My father vowed that he could not support two churches, my mother, who was Methodist, joined the Methodist church before she married my father. The Methodist Church always did an Easter program and all children were expected to learn parts of a poem or speeches to be recited at the program.

My first speech was two or three lines of a short Easter poem, of which we all read a portion. "Easter lilies, pure and sweet, spread them all beneath our feet." We were to courtesy and depart the stage showing off our new dresses, socks and shoes. We dressed in our "Sunday best," sewn by sister, Pearl. This particular time we wore pongee dresses, trimmed in pink, patent leather black slippers, and pink socks. Our hair was neatly primped, our large braids on top, two on each side. We had to be careful with our dresses and shoes because we had to walk a mile to get to the church, no "horseplay" along the way. After church they had to be carefully put away until the next occasion to be worn.

Some Sunday was reserved after the regular service to have "dinner on the grounds. Families would come to church with their wagons loaded with all kinds of food to have a feast after church. Each family placed their baskets on a long table under large oaks and sweet gum trees to share with their neighbors. There was plenty of fried chicken, turnip greens, peas a few vegetables that did not spoil easily with pies of all kinds of cakes of many flavors. To be washed down with soda water in barrels or tubs of ice.

This was a special time for children to play after being "cooped up" in church. Playing tag was the main game as long as their Sunday best was not soiled, call "Sunday Clothes" otherwise they had to be prepared to find a "switch" and pay for their carelessness.

HISTORY OF MT. PISGAH BAPTIST CHURCH 1960

By: Laura V. Shavers

I have been asked to give the history of the church. To attempt such is indeed a great pleasure. Not that I feel that I can do justice to the subject, but because this is an institution of God, created by Him and instituted for the purpose of carrying out His divine plan. And there is something within me I cannot explain that makes me very anxious to do something for the forwarding of His cause. "Something within me I cannot explain. Something within me that holdeth the rain. All that I know, there is something within".

We find the first church was organized on the day of Pentecost. Man's nature has changed but little since Christ was on earth. Man is an imperfect being. The church that came into existence on the day of Pentecost was a perfect institution because God was behind it. Imperfect man has tampered with the church through ages past, therefore it has imperfections today.

No matter what man has done to hinder, the church moves on. We find it stronger in number, purer in faith, more zealous than it has been since the days of the apostasy.

There are many churches, many faiths and equally as many different congregations, to the extent we shall attempt to name but only a few.

If I were to tell you about the apostolic church I would take it from the mouth of the Apostle Paul.

If I were to tell you about the Roman Catholic Church I would refer you to the Pope.

We would think of William Penn as head of the Puritan church. Roger Williams as head of the Baptist church, Chas. Wesley, the Methodist church, and on and on it goes. But I am to tell you about a missionary Baptist church in Garland Community organized about the year of 1950.

A very short time before 1850 there came into this community a Mr. Jack Garland who had many slaves. This man was said to be a devout Christian and taught his slaves the Christian way of life. He gave to them (the slaves) land to construct a building for worship. Both Methodist and Baptist worshiped in this building under the leadership and first deacon Anthony Garland.

There were many pastors. Many could read, but…little. We will name a few: Moses Conse, Sam Whitfield, Silas Davis, Frank Hughes, Genter James Riley and Ephrin Dunlap.

Under Dunlap our church obtained a plot of ground from Anthony Garland and erected its first church building, and left the original land and church given by Mr. Garland to the Methodist.

Our second building was erected about 1900 when Rev. Rogers was pastor. This building burned in about 1915. Then under Rev. Sexton's second election another building was erected. Our debt remained unpaid for many years. Rev. Hopkins was pastor when the last note was paid during the Depression. Mr. Whybock was very liberal and accepted only one third.

Many pastors would come and go, some very good, some less useful. We must pay special tribute to Rev. Forte. We loved him because he loved us. He passed away as a pastor of this church. He was elected for two terms. Our present pastor's Bro. L.W. Woods. Words are inadequate to express our gratefulness to him for his untiring and eloquent leadership. We hope for him the best afforded to mankind.

We must say that we bestowed upon the women of this church much credit for all that has been achieved, for they have gone shoulder to shoulder with the men and oftentimes a shoulder above.

These are the deacons, as we recall: Anthony Garland (the first), Henry Pickey, Albert King, Nathan Ducket, Iverson Shavers, Payton Bruce Fetherson, Alonzo McClellan, Tom Bell, Tom Newton, John Garth, John Germany, Charley Haynes, John Satewhite, Marshall Sherman, Ben Estes, Lorenzo Shavers, Perlie Mills, Anderson Stephens, William Barber and Ed Hooks are on trial. These men with few exceptions have filled the requirement as a deacon. And now my dear congregation we would like for you to see us as we really are. We still possess the ties of our ancestors.

We purpose to be true, for there are those who trust us. We must live true, for there are those who care. We must be strong for there are those who suffer. We must be brave for there is much to dare".

The Masonic Hall and the Heroins

There were two other organizations in the community that were very important during the late 1800s, the Masons and the Heroins. The Masonic Hall was one of the first buildings located near the Baptist Church and the first one seen on the road to the left about 2½ miles after entering the community from Highway 82. It was a large structure two stories high.

The main level was often used for church services and as a fellowship hall, especially after the Baptist Church burned.

Many of the same individuals who were active in the schools were also Masons. They were the decision makers in the community – Christian leaders of justice for the underdog. Heroins were also Christian leaders with codes of service and justice.

As a child, I was reluctant to even pass by the building; children were not allowed to be alone in the building. We were told that it was haunted and that in order to be a member, we had to ride a goat.

The organizations were a great source of camaraderie and support for the community and human justice. The two story structure finally burned and many of the men left or moved – also the women. But when the building burned it frighten one of my sisters so she almost went into shock and had to be put to bed (we lived just down the lane and saw it all).

I shall never forget the big "barrel" of tar that was placed outside of the building; for the purpose of repairing the roof. Sometimes children passed by and dug out a piece (they didn't know the danger). "It was just a great chew, they thought."

What is a history of "The Heroines of Jericho"?

The Heroines of Jericho was a degree that was conferred on women related to Mason, including wives, mothers, sisters, widows, and daughters. The course was designed to instruct women on high and noble principles "to appeal to the better instincts of the human mind." The symbol of the Heroines is a spinning wheel and they consider Rahab, Ruth, and Mary to be among their heroes. When a male receives a similar degree, he is considered a Knight of Jericho.
Note: See Appendix Reference: www.hoj701.org.

Homes in Garland

During the late 1800's and early 1900's when cotton was still "King" the people in Garland were able to have large homes but no electricity or running water. They used coal oil lamps and well or spring water, some used cistern water. A few were able to buy cars (T-Model). They had inherited land from their forefathers who were slaves and inherited land from their masters. At that time they could work their farms raising mostly cotton and corn to buy enough seeds and fertilizer for the next year and buy a wagon and team, build a large house, send their children to school. This all changed after the "crash" in 1929.

Many people lost their farms, wagons and teams; banks closed and one could not borrow money. A few people in Garland were able to hang on but never fully recovered. My family had just built a home and that year had one of the coldest winters of all time. While the house was being built we had to walk home from a cousin's house about a mile away each morning and back again in the evening.

Sharing in a time of change was key to survival. The homes at that time were built of weather boarding material but most had fire places and pot-bellied stoves to keep warm. Children wore union wear and high top shoes. Woe unto you if you forgot to button the flap in the back or forgot to unbutton up after going to the rest room or an accident could occur and there were no extras until returning home. The experience was challenging but kept one "on his/her toes," especially when one had only one change. Change is always good; we survived.

Road in Garland Community

One of the roads that passed through the pine forest by my grandfather's home was frightful at night time. One could hardly see one's own hands before one's face at night. Not a place to be at night!

On the main road just off highway 82W, leading into the community (Garland), there was an area just past Jim Garland Lane that possessed a phenomenal spot one did not wish to pass through after dark. For reasons unknown, whenever an animal passed through that spot, it would become very agitated. If riding in a wagon, the horses pulling the wagon would balk or rear-up and it was difficult to control them or hold their reigns . . . a place of fright! Even in recent years, a man and his wife riding on a motorcycle, met head on with a horse standing in the middle of that road. As you might imagine, the result was fata.

Hog Jaw Road was lined at one time with thick trees and bushes, and it was dark as "pitch." It was said to be an area where wild hogs roamed. If walking this road late at night, one took the liberty to "run like the wind," or sing loudly enough for all neighbors to know someone was on that road.

Roads Leading to Family Homes and Farms to Market Services

The main road that ran through Garland community about four miles plus or minus ran from DeKalb like a strip of land which could have easily been called the "strip" from DeKalb to Oak Grove and Avery. During the early 1900s this road was like a wagon trail road mostly ungraveled – just raw earth. Many wagons had been bogged in the mire and required expert assistance to unbog them. Later years when cars were used for travel, they too got stuck and had to be released from the red clay bog or hazard. After World War II roads began to be paved and travel became easier. Outside of deep country way fairs most of the road leading to or around Garland Community are now paved and it is more convenient to visit the neighbors. A little late for "Farm to Market" convenience, "a dream delayed" or deferred unrealized during the early 1900s.

Roads or lanes in Garland and surrounding areas – Garland main roads, Route 2, the Jim Garland Lane, Hog Jaw Road, and Lydia Road, Betts Village Road; others named by numbers as farm roads.

One of the most interesting stories is about the road call "Hog Jaw" which is told in another section of this book.

Transportation

Most of the inhabitants in Garland Community walked to their destination or if able to afford it, rode in a buggy, one horse soe8gh,"jitty." A car was ...was rare or non-existent during the first generation. My father walked twelve miles or more to attend school or rode a horse. He was determined to get an education and after high school, attended Fisk University after returning home around 1904, then taught school.

EDUCATION AND SCHOOLS

Education has been a priority in the lives of Ruth's children since the second generation. Ruth's father encouraged education. He and his family took the lead in establishing schools after slavery. Ruth's son, Robert Garland, was one of the first teachers in Garland. He had been taught by his mother before education had been encouraged. I can remember during the late 1920's or early 1930's, seeing Robert's picture hanging in the entrance corridor in the Garland high school along with some other pictures of white teachers or trustees.

Education is one of the driving cultural forces in any community; it aids in motivating individuals within those communities to become healthy, strong, and productive beings. This section demonstrates how Garland Community developed through believing in education and having a strong educational system which set as its goal that of educating its citizens and future leaders. Public or community education serves as an important tool for upgrading literacy in any population, thus encouraging a better quality of life through improved communication and understanding.

Allotted to slaves after the Civil War
Subsistence after the Civil War

The inhabitants of this community lived or obtained their food and shelter from the bounty of the land. There was the abundance of natural fruits, nuts and vegetation to sustain most people during the summer and fall to keep them alive and reasonably healthy. If they formed their small allotted piece of land and had saved a few pennies they could preserve their food for winter. There was enough wood to use for burning to keep them warm in a fireplace and cooking in the large iron pots stationed over the coals or beneath the asher, mainly potatoes, corn or dried food, peas, beans, "shocked" peanuts or banked turnips or collards. Some were able to preserve the garden vegetables by "canning." Careful planning was essential for survival. No fancy clothing – most saved a few pennies to buy cloth at 5 or 10 cents a yard to make clothing sewing by hand or by machine which was very rare. Quilts and bedding were made from the downs of geese or chicken feathers if available. The quilts were from the flour or feed sacks for clothing. Hay was gathered and stored for animals. Pigs were fed from left over dishwater called "slop" and occasionally from corn or mush. Corn was taken to a mill to be ground into meal for a small fee 5 or 10 cents.

Housing was meager or deficient; insulated with whatever was available. They kept their windows open in the summer if they had them or opened and propped their shutters with a stick or pole. Their kitchens were large but with very small storage under dirt floors faced with hard clay with perhaps a "safe" for dishes, a stove and side boards for panels for holding cooking utensils. The iron stand used wood for cooking and sometimes to keep the whole house warm in winter. The canning was done outside. During the early morning about 5 o'clock before the cock crowed and one could hear the ringing of the ax and splitting of the block of wood or chopping of lumber to cook the breakfast or to start the fire for the family to keep warm after arising from the night's sleep. If lucky, breakfast consisted of hot biscuits, thick jowl bacon, biscuits and syrup. If one had accumulated coins, there may be butter, churned before breakfast to eat with the biscuits and syrup and butter milk to drink. Maybe clabber the next day if the cream had risen and had been skimmed off for churning. Many of the inhabitants died from tuberculosis and other diseases. There were only two doctors in DeKalb and there were no inoculations available or shots to ward off disease. Most mothers nursed their children; a natural way to acquire some immunity from some diseases. Longevity was rare beyond 65. A few lived to be over 80+. This can be verified if one visits the cemetery and reads at the date of birth and date of death.

Cleanliness and Hygiene

The inhabitants learned to make their own soap, made from the fat from pigs (lard) and lye or ashes. This was made for washing clothes or bathing. If one could afford a can of lye or knew how to separate the ashes and used the settled fluid he could make his own soap.

The History of Public Education in Texas

An Overview

Texans have long been concerned about the education of their children. The Texas Declaration of Independence in 1836 listed the failure of the **Mexican** government "to establish any public system of education, although possessed of almost boundless resources…" among the reasons for severing political ties with Mexico.

The first Anglo-American public school law in Texas was exacted in 1840 and provided for surveying and setting aside four leagues (17,712 acres) off and in each county to support public schools. Later, the state constitution of 1845 provided that one tenth of the annual State tax revenue be set aside as a perpetual fund to support free public schools.

In 1845, a new school law set aside as a permanent school fund $2 million of the million in five percent U.S. Indemnity bonds received in settlement of Texas' boundary claims against the United States.

After the Civil War and Reconstruction, the new state constitution of 1876 set aside 45 million acres of public domain for school support and directed that the income from the new Permanent School Fund be invested in bonds.

Slaveholder's dominated the state's economic and political life. The government of the Republic of Texas and, after 1845, the state legislature passed a series of slave codes to regulate the behavior of slaves and restrict the rights of free blacks.

When rumors of a slave insurrection circulated in the state in 1860, Texas virtually suspended civil liberties and due process in the state. Suspected abolitionists were expelled from the state, and one was even hanged. A vigilante group in Dallas lynched three African-American slaves who were suspected of starting a fire that burnt most of the downtown area. Other slaves in the county were whipped.

The Texas vote for secession in February 1861 hastened the end of slavery and set in motion the eventual liberation of the state's African American population. For Blacks in Texas, Freedom did not come until Juneteenth, June 19, 1865. In contrast to other parts of the South, where the approach of the Union Army encouraged thousands of enslaved blacks to free themselves and run away, Texas blacks remained enslaved until the end of the Civil War. Few were able to run away and enlist in the Union Army, as black men did in other parts of the South.

The Reconstruction era presented black Texas another challenge. Many had to rebuild their lives, locate lost family members, and begin to live their lives as self-sufficient, free men and women. The establishment of the Freedmen's Bureau in the state aided this transition from slavery to freedom. But given the continuing racial animosity that separated blacks and whites after the war, this was not an easy task. The state legislature and several Texas cities passed Black Codes to restrict the rights of blacks, to prevent them from having free access to public facilities, and to force them back to the rural areas as agricultural laborers. The use of the political and legal system to regulate black behavior was accompanied by a literal reign of terror in the state. From 1865 to 1868 white Texans committed over 1, 500 acts of violence against blacks; more than 350 blacks were murdered by whites. These were social organizations to serve their own needs. They established newspapers (the *Dallas* Express, *Houston Informer and Texas Freeman*, and San Antonio *Register*), grocery stores, funeral homes and other business establishments that served a predominant African-American clientele. In the late nineteenth century black farmers founded **a** cooperative to encourage black land ownership and to raise crop prices. From 1900 to 1940 a majority of black Texans remained **in** farming, with about 20 percent owning their land while most rented farms **as** tenants. The Great Depression of the 1930s hastened **a** trend toward urbanization. In the **same** period blacks **in** Dallas organized a cotton-processing mill, but it failed in less than five years. These self-help and economic development efforts by black Texans indicate that they did not allow the oppression of white racism to deter them from striving to build successful communities. After the Civil War, African Americans also developed their first educational institutions. Black colleges such as Bishop, Paul Quinn and Wiley were founded by several religious denominations, primarily Baptist and Methodist organizations. African-Americans churches such **as** Boll Street African Methodist Episcopal in Dallas also started the first schools in that city for black children. The city of Houston provided schools for its black citizens beginning in 1871. By 1888 the city government **in** Dallas followed suit– brought a modicum of safety to African Americans. The arrival of military and Congressional efforts to protect black rights ushered in the second phase of Reconstruction in the state. In this period African Americans made a substantial contribution to the transition of Texas from a slave-labor state to one based on free labor. Ten African-American delegates at the Constitutional Convention of 1868-1869 helped to write a constitution that protected civil rights, established the state's first public education system, and extended the franchise to all men. Between 1868 and 1900, forty-three African Americans served in the state legislature, and they helped to move the state toward democracy.

FREEMEN'S BUREAU:

The Bureau of Refugees, Freedmen, and Abandoned Lands, commonly known as the Freedmen's Bureau, was established by Congress in March 1865 as a branch of the United States Army. It was to be a temporary agency. Its functions were to provide relief to the thousands of refugees, black and white, who had been left homeless by the Civil War; to supervise affairs related to newly freed slaves in the southern states; and to administer all land abandoned by Confederates or confiscated from them during the war.

The bureau was most successful in its educational effort. At the end of 1865, sixteen schools were serving just over 1,000 black pupils. By July of 1870, the last month of the bureau's activities, 150 schools enrolled 9,086 black students. As in other areas of their work, the bureau had faced fierce and determined opposition on the part of some white Texans, who burned school buildings, harassed teachers, and otherwise obstructed progress. Gradually, however, the opposition declined. In his last report, the superintendent of the Texas schools reported that "The burning of school houses and — maltreatment of teachers so common at the commencement of the Bureau operations, have almost entirely ceased." Even historians generally critical of the Freedmen's Bureau have conceded that the education of blacks in Texas would not have been possible so soon without its efforts. See also **AFRICAN AMERICANS and SLAVERY.**

Ref. Handbook of Texas Online "Freedmen's Bureau" www.TSH...

ARTICLE X. — EDUCATION

SECTION 1: A general diffusion of knowledge being essential to the preservation of the rights and liberties of the people, it shall be the duty of the Legislature of this State to make suitable provisions for the support and maintenance of public schools.

SECTION 2: The Legislature shall, as early as practicable, establish a system of free schools throughout the State; and as a basis for the endowment and support of said system, all the funds , lands and other property heretofore set apart and appropriated, or that may hereafter be set apart and appropriated for the support and maintenance of public schools, shall constitute the public school fund; and said fund, and the income derived there from, shall be a perpetual fund exclusively for the education of all the white scholastic inhabitants of this State, and no law shall ever be made appropriating said fund to any other use or purpose whatever. And until such time as the Legislature shall provide for the establishment of such system of public schools in the State, the fund thus created and the income derived there from, shall remain as a charge against the State, and be passed to the credit of the free common school fund.

SECTION 3: And all the alternate sections of land reserved by the State out of grants heretofore made, or that may hereafter be made, to railroad companies or other corporations of any nature whatever, for internal improvements, or for the development of the wealth and resources of the State, shall be set apart as a part of the perpetual school fund of the State; provided, that if at any time hereafter any portion of the public domain of this State shall be sold, and by virtue of said sale the jurisdiction over said land shall be vested in the United States Government, in such event one half of the proceeds derived from said sale -"" shall become a part of the perpetual school fund of the State; and the Legislature shall hereafter appropriate one half of the proceeds resulting from all sales of the public lands to the perpetual public school fund.

SECTION 4: The Legislature shall provide, from time to time, for the sale of lands belonging to the perpetual public school fund, upon such time and terms as it may deem expedient; provided, that in cases of sale the preference shall be given to actual settlers; and, provided further, that the Legislature shall have no power to grant relief to purchasers by granting further time for payment, but shall in all cases, provide for the forfeiture of the land to the State for the benefit of a perpetual public school fund; and that all interest accruing upon such sales shall be apart of the income belonging to the school fund, and subject to appropriation annually for educational purposes.

SECTION 5: The Legislature shall have no power to appropriate or loan or invest, except as follows, any part of the principal sum of the perpetual school full for any purpose whatever; and it shall be the duty of the Legislature to appropriate annually the income which may derive from said fund, for educational purposes, under such system as it may adopt; and it shall, from time to time, cause the principal sum now on hand and arising from sales of land, or from any other source to be invested in the bond of the United States of America, or the bonds of the State of Texas, or such bonds as the State my guarantee.

SECTION 6: All public lands which have been heretofore, or may be hereafter, granted for public schools, to the various counties or other political divisions in this State, shall be under the control of the Legislature, and may be sold on such terms and under such regulations as the Legislature shall be law prescribed; and the proceeds of the sale of said lands shall be added to the perpetual school fund of the State. But each without the consent of such county or counties to which the lands may belong.

SECTION 7: The Legislature may provide for the levying of a tax for educational purposes; provided, the taxes levied shall be distributed from year to year, as the same may be collected; and provided, that all the sums arising from said tax which may be collected from Africans, or persons of African descent, shall be exclusively appropriated for the maintenance of a system of public schools for Africans and their children; and it shall be the duty of the Legislature to encourage schools among these people.

SECTION 8: The moneys and lands heretofore granted to, or which may hereafter be granted for the endowment and support of one or more universities, shall constitute a special fund for the maintenance of said universities, and until the university or universities are located and commenced, the principal and the interest arising from the investment of the principal, shall be invested in like manner, and under the same restrictions as provided for the investment and control of the perpetual public school fund~ in Sections four and five (4 and 5) in this Article of the Constitution, and the Legislature shall have no power to appropriate the university fund for an early day, make such provisions, by law, as will organize and put into operation the university.

SECTION 9: The four hundred thousand acres of land that have been surveyed and set apart, under the provisions of a law approved 30th August, A. D. 1856, for the benefit of a Lunatic Asylum, a Deaf and Dumb Asylum, a Blind Asylum, and an Orphan Asylum, shall constitute a fund for the support of such institutions, one fourth of each, and the said fund shall never be diverted to any other purpose. The —said lands may be sold, and the fund invested under the same rules and regulations as provided for the lands belonging to the school fund. The income of said fund only shall be applied to the support of such institutions; and until so applied, shall be invested in the same manner as the principal.

SECTION 10: The Governor, by and with the advice and consent of two-thirds of the Senate~ shall appoint an officer to be styled the Superintendent of Public Instruction. His term of office shall be four years, and his annual salary shall not be less than ($2,000) two thousand dollars, payable at stated times; and the Governor, Comptroller and Superintendent of Public Education shall constitute a Board to be styled a Board of Education, and shall have the general management and control of the perpetual school fund, and common schools, under such regulations as the Legislature may hereafter prescribe.

SECTION 11: The several counties in this State which have not received their quantum of the lands for the purposes of education, shall be entitled to the same quantity heretofore appropriated by the Congress of the Republic of Texas, and the State, to other counties. And the counties which have not had the lands to which they are entitled for educational purposes, located, shall have the right to contract for the location, surveying and procuring the patents for said lands, and of paying for the same with any portion of said lands so patented, not to exceed one fourth of the whole amount to be so located, surveyed and patented to be divided according to quality, allowing to each part a fair proportion of land, water and timber.

Constitution of the State of Texas (1866) -

ROBERT GARLAND

THE FIRST BLACK TEACHER IN GARLAND COMMUNITY TAUGHT BY HIS MOTHER, JENNY KNIGHT

Professor Major Johnson

The first black teacher in Garland with a formal education who taught the author's mother. Each time Professor Johnson visited my Mother, the author was requested to take care of him.

It has been documented that John Garland was a strong believer in education. Many of his slaves could read and write. It appears that he came from a family that believed in education; one of his relatives, I am told, may have been the first chancellor of Vanderbilt University in Nashville, Tennessee. His name was Landon C. Garland, 1875-1893. Another relative was the governor of Arkansas. This ancestor had arrived from England in the early 1700s, in Virginia and moving through North Carolina to Tennessee. Many Garlands are now scattered throughout the nation. A list of Garlands is presented in the appendices from the archives of Tennessee located in Nashville. A genealogical search was completed by Mrs. Laverne White in October 2002 as a labor of love and respect.

The formal profession of many of Ruth's children was teaching. Immediately after the Civil War of the 1860s most of Ruth's children were farmers, with a sprinkling of self-proclaimed preachers, orators, abolitionist, mid-wives, and those self-learned teachers. As time passed, when colleges or places of secondary education were developed for blacks, many took advantage of them.

Major Johnson, head teacher or principal taught for many years in Garland; he taught many members of the third generation of Garlands during the late 1800s. He had earned a teaching certificate diploma at either Bishop College in Marshall, Texas or at Fisk College (now Fisk University) in Nashville, TN or at Howard University in Washington, DC. During the early years, there were few if any schools for blacks that were developed at the secondary or graduate level.

Mr. Jackson, Music Teacher, Garland High School

Early in September of the year approximately 1930, a young man arrived in Garland Community to teach music and also to teach the fifth grade. In October of that year, a program was presented and he played before the school audience. One of his selections was entitled "The Jingaboo Mann." The whole audience was in awe as his nimble fingers tickled the key board with a introductory sound, weird and mournful, and then he began to sing:

One night when I was walking across the meadow
just about a mile from home,
twas then I heard a rustle in the bushes,
and then I heard a low, low moan.
I started for my maw's house a-crying
And round the house, you should have seen me go.
But when I reached the door,
To my Mami I did go
I said, 'Ma, I saw the shadow of the Jingaboo.
He's got great big shiny eyes
He's got a great big mouth this size,
He looks like this and that
He eats up the children
both lean and fat.
He goes out all through the night,
He is dressed in nothing but white
Run! Run! Run! Just as fast as you can,
and hide yourself away from
That ole' Jingaboo man!

The author of this song has never been found. Credit is given to one who performed it: Professor Jackson, teacher of music, Garland High School, DeKalb, Texas, 1930

Whenever this song crosses my mind, a cold chill runs up and down my spine as it did when I was a child hearing it for the first time. The memory of Professor Jackson singing it is awesome. A ghost dressed in white startles my very being as I see it chasing little children who run for their very lives to find some protection in the pitch black night. Then I come to my senses and know that this is only a song.

Schools

The first formally organized school in Garland Community was opened after the Civil War. The Rosenwald Funds became available later. The principal or head teacher was a Mr. Winston.

The earlier schools were located near churches in the community of the homes or vacant houses. Some of the pictures and names of students are listed in the appendices and are listed in the report written by Dr. Raynard Kington when gathering information for the National Register for Historic Places.

It has been documented by clippings from the archives in Clarksville, Texas and Nashville, Tennessee that John C. Garland was a strong believer in education. The Garland Community School was better organized and educated more students who have received the highest degrees in education than other areas throughout the county, than any other community in East Texas.

Wert Garland and some of the other Garlands played an important role in helping some of Ruth's great grandchildren secure jobs, especially in the teaching profession. Wert Garland had great influence in the surrounding communities. Whenever vacancies became available or a parent whose child had credentials, he could seek out Wert Garland for help in seeking that job and usually that person was able to be hired because Wert Garland had spoken for him/her (see article about Wert Garland).

Texas

3030

3030

Garland School, Texas

Bowie County 3030

Eighteen acres of land

Three-teacher type + 2 R... = 5 T

Built under the 1923-24 budget 1927-28

Application No. 23-C

Total cost	$3,400	+ 2100 = 5500
Negroes	$500.00	+ 1050 = 1550
Whites		
Public	2,000.00	+ 750 2750
Rosenwald	900.00	+ 300 1200

MR. R.S. PIC

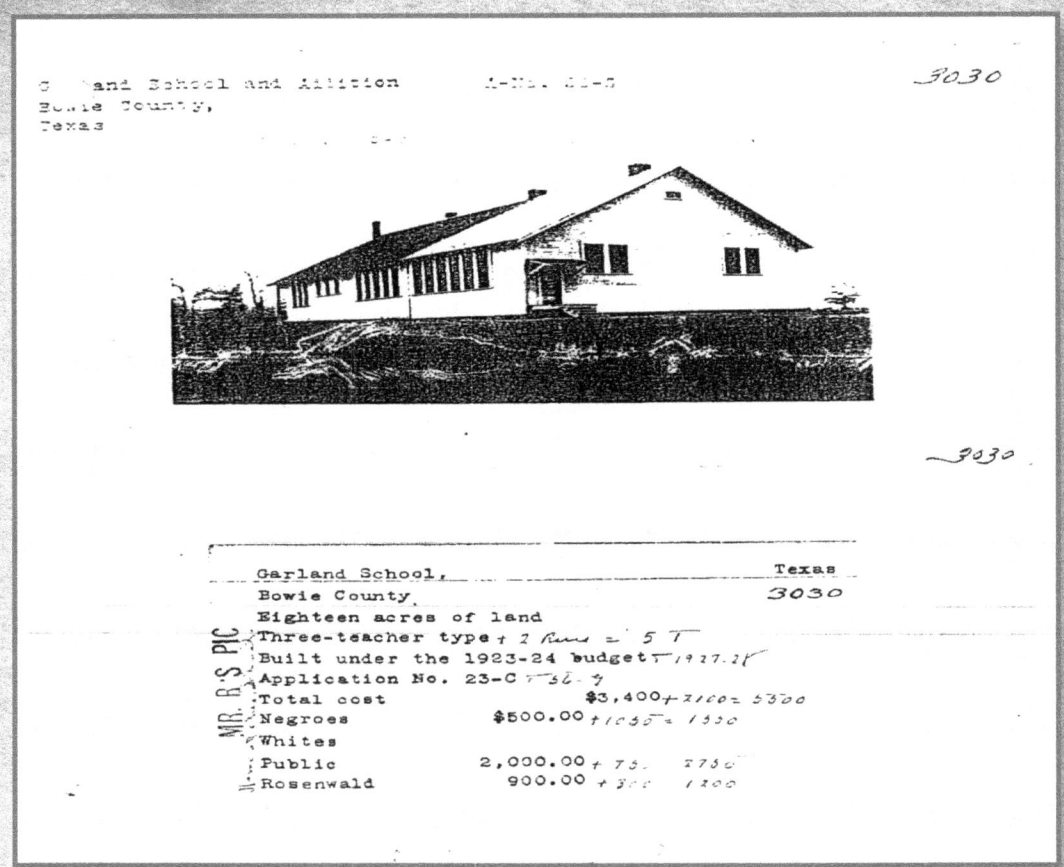

Garland Common School District No. 9
March 15, 1936

By L.H. Griffin
(Research by "U.S. McClelian")

This school is located about four miles west of DeKalb and about one mile from Highway 7. This is probably the oldest exclusive Negro district in Bowie County. The last scholastic census showed that only three white families resided in this district, and since no white school is maintained in the district, these children attend the DeKalb public schools.

This district is in one of the poorest belts of upland farming territory, and there is very little income except from agriculture-products. This community was established soon after the Civil War and many are the pleasant memories that have been recalled by white citizens who happen to be passing through the community at meal time or at night, of the hospitality of Ben Garland, one of the early founders of this community. He kept a room prepared at his home for the convenience of any white traveler who might happen to be there at night time. He always considered it a privilege to extend the hospitality of his home to any white citizen who might be traveling that way. He never took pay for the excellent meals served at his home or the bed that was furnished, for he said he liked to serve his good friends of the white race. He probably had more white friends in Bowie County than any Negro that has ever lived in the county. This Negro school was founded and developed by a Negro citizen of the same high type as Ben Garland.

The history of this district falls into three natural chronological periods—the first of which was from 1875 to 1880. During this period the school was taught in succession by four white men from the north, namely "Nimrod" (1) Winston, Fate Ingram, a Mr. Byrd, and Mr. Johnson. Their salaries were paid by subscriptions from the patrons of the school and were of necessity very small. It is highly probable that they received some reimbursement from the northern society that sent them. The building used was a one room crudely constructed log house, located on the plot of ground where the Garland Methodist Church now stands. The building had no teaching equipment at all and the furniture was of the simplest type and included split log benches. The playground was not even cleared off and the children played in the woods surrounding the building. Even crude playground equipment was unheard of then. The building and equipment were valued at $60.00, a very liberal estimate at that.

The second period was from 1880 to 1892, at which the school district was organized for the community. The teachers for this period were selected by the county Superintendent and were all Negros. They were in order of service: Robert Garland, David Kenley, John Stout, Myrtle Vaughn, and Don Davis. The building used was the same one that was used in the preceding period and it might be said in passing that the equipment was still wholly lacking. The school term ranged from two to three months in length and the salaries were $25.00 to $35.00 per month.

From 1892 to 1935 is the third period and we find the county forming the Garland school district No. 9. In 1904 the Negro Methodist church was used as a school building and in 1902 a one room boxed house was built near the present school building and the next year another room of similar construction was added. The principal M.J. Johnson had in mind to make this an industrial school. The citizens of the community supported the project and 32 acres of land were purchased. Johnson served the district from 1902 to 1910 and during this time his assistant teachers were in order of service: Mrs. Ada Garland Davis, Mrs. T.E.Y. Pollard, Mrs. Willie Franklin, Mrs. Lola B. Elmore, and Robert S. Shavers. The first three teachers were Robert Garland, Aurtie Garland, F.J. Garland, A.L. Mclelian, Jessie Garland, W.B. Garland succession of head teachers and assistant teachers, Durilla Johnson (1910-1911), teacher Mrs. Lewis, and Mrs. Swink, C.A. Barrett, (1913-1915), assistant teacher Mrs. L.V. Shavers and Mrs. Susie Swink. E.L. Muckleroy, (1915-17), assistant teachers Lillilian Garland and Cora Waller, F.W. Mills (1920-21), assistant teachers Lillian Garland, F.W. Green (1921-23), assistant teachers Lillian Dickerson, and Almenia Hackney.

U.S. McClelian has been principal continuously since 1923 and his assistant teachers have been Lillian Dickerson, Almenia Hackney, Mrs. S.L. McClelian, Rebecca Howard, Mattie Nunley, Mrs. Hinnegan, Mrs. Alaska Walker, Mrs. Francis Sands, M. A. J. Garland, E. W. Herron, and Travis Downs. During this time the trustees who have served are A.L. McClelian, Charles W. Haynes, C.H. Garland, V.B. Berry, J.D. Waller, J.F. Sharp, Robert S. Shavers, John L. Garth, Joe B. Betts, S.L. McClelian, and William Wyatt.

This school has made an enviable record for service to the students of the community. Thirty-one teachers have been trained in this school and have taken their place in the teaching world. The large percentage of them at present is employed in the Bowie County schools in addition to teachers, the school members among the ex-students: one missionary, one social worker, one physician, one research worker, in the U.S. Department of Education, an undertaker and embalmer. This has been possible only through the excellent co-operation between the homes of the community and the school.

At present a four-year accredited school employing five teachers is maintained in the district. The school has been granted sixteen units of affiliation by the State Department of Education and is reorganized as a Class A high school. The building is a six room frame building of Rosanwald type; near the school building is a modern six room teacherage also owned by the district. The equipment is one of the very latest types and includes a fairly well equipped manual training department. A very conservative estimate places the value of the building at $4500, and the equipment at $2500.

The district is very small containing only six square miles with a property valuation of $33,780, and a local tax rate of $.50 for bond and $.50 for local maintenance. There are 40 families containing 127 scholastic *(2)* that reside in the district.

The Historical Significance of the Garland Community Rosenwald Teacherage

The Garland community was founded in Bowie County, approximately four miles west of DekAlb, shortly after the Civil War when John Calhoun Garland either deeded or sold at reduced rates land to his former slaves, some of whom were his direct offspring. The land was used to create homesteads and community institutions including a school, a cemetery, and two churches. Garland had come to Texas from Tennessee with his family and slaves in the 1850's. Accordingly to oral histories, he earned a reputation as a relatively liberal slave master in that he kept families intact and circumvented existing Texas laws by allowing some of his slaves to learn to read and write. The Garland community school was founded in 1875 in a crude log house and was initially staffed entirely by white teachers from Northern missionary societies, one of whom, Nimrod Winston, married one of Garland's daughters. Within ten years of its founding, the school came under County supervision and by the 1880's its teachers were all African American. In the early 1890's, the county formerly created the Garland School District No. 9, and in 1902, the first one-room school house was built. Between 1923 and 1924, with the support of the Rosenwald Fund and with contributions from the county and the black citizens of the community, the final Garland school and a teacherage were constructed.

The Garland school was extraordinarily successful viewed in the context of the status of most African Americans in the South at that time. It had an excellent reputation for the quality of its educational instruction, and when a brief history of the school district was written in the 1930's, it employed five teachers and had achieved a Class A rating for its high school. Even at that time, the Garland school sent a significant percentage of its graduates on to the historically black colleges and universities and regularly produced students who entered the professions and went on to become important community leaders. The school district was unique in that much of the land in the community was owned by the descendants of the Garland slaves, who were thus significantly more independent than African Americans in many other parts of Texas. Furthermore, there were few white families who lived in the district, and those who were there sent their children to school in DeKalb. As a result, the African American community members in Garland, in their roles as trustees, obtained substantial independence in the oversight of the school district, which contributed to its success.

The teacherage played an important role in the success of the school district by providing essential housing to the teachers who were recruited to this school district. Because of its rural location and the rigid residential segregation of the time, there were few housing options for African American teachers who came to Garland, many of whom were single women. The teacherage, located behind the school, which was in turn close to the Garland church and store, became a center of the community.

The Garland School was consolidated with the Marvin Pynes School in DeKalb in the 1950's and was for many years used as a community center. It was demolished several years ago after many years of neglect and deterioration. The teacherage was purchased by descendants of the original founders of the community and has not been occupied for over ten years.

THE CEMETERY

After the blooming
of
each flower
Nature claims its own
to earth
and the changing
of
each hour
Brings the sunlight
from
Shadows blight
and the call
to
Each His service
is the way
to
Journey's light
For the flower that blooms
in summer
is
A promise of God's might!

History of Garland Community Cemetery

By Laura Pearl Shavers Sands

Under History of Cemeteries Garland Cemetery in Annona, TX
L to R -- Iverson Shavers marker of John C. Garland Mattie Shavers Johnson

The Cemetery

There were two cemeteries for the descendant of Col. John C. Garland and the Garlands left on the plantation in Garland Community. There is a cemetery in Ted River County which contains the white descendants of Col. Garland. The second cemetery is located in Garland Community in DeKalb, Texas. It contains the descendants of the slaves from the Garland Plantation. The following history was recorded by Laura Pearl Shavers Sands.

The history of Garland Community Cemetery is a history of the people who have lived in Garland Community. It is 100 years old or older, this year (1987). The monument of Judy Garland, age 60, marks the place where, according to word-of-mouth, the first person was buried in this cemetery. Other earliest dates, on monuments, are those of Tom Garland and J. Swink – both died in 1887. Jim Garland, Ruth Garland's husband, was buried earlier, but no one seems to know the date. There is no monument on his grave.

Between the years of 1836 and 1852, the Garland families from Madison County, Tennessee moved to DeKalb, Texas bringing slaves with them who were the families of Ben and Permelia Garland, Anthony and Mary Garland, and Jim and Ruth Garland, Alfred and Candice, brother and sister of Anthony Garland, and many more came, also.

Here, about three miles west of DeKalb a plantation of master and slaves was established which was finally to be known as Garland Community with its churches, public school, a cemetery, and a post office named Booker.

Nimrod Winston, a son-in-law of Col. John C. Garland, and Robert Garland were the first Garland Community public school teachers following the Reconstruction Period – after the Civil War (see study in Bowie County Schools Supt. Office). After the Civil War, the former slave owners moved to Red River County leaving on the land the above named slaves who finally secured deeds to the land upon which they dwelled.

Land abstracts indicated that the land of the slave owner in Garland did not make before his death will nor deeds to his heirs, for anything he owned in DeKalb. Later partition deeds were "drawn-up" and recorded in the Bowie County Courthouse. According to word-of-mouth, this courthouse was destroyed by fire in about 1900, and some of the records may not have been re-recorded.

It was generally believed that the Garland slave owners or their heirs donated to Garland Community a track of land which was for two churches (one Methodist and one Baptist) combined with a public school, and another one (track of land) for a cemetery.

A deed in Bowie County Courthouse in Book 53, page 412 --- Showing that a track of land had been granted to the Methodist Church South has been recorded and available for viewing. No one was certain about the deed to the cemetery until one was found, recorded at the courthouse, showing that the late Mollie Garland-Whitmore, a former wife of Joe Ben Garland, 1865-1911, reserved for herself a lifetime use of the cemetery, and for her heirs, a burial place (see deed in Bowie County Courthouse).

Many, other than the Garland families, have moved to Garland Community and have used the cemetery as a place to bury their deceased.

Please, review the family trees of Col. John C. Garland, Ben and Permelia Garland, and many others that may give a better understanding of the history of Garland Community located west of DeKalb on Oak Grove Road, between Hwy. 1701 and Hwy. 82 west of and adjacent to an old Indian burial ground.

Cemeteries

The layout of the cemetery in Garland Community is located in the files of Laura P. Sands. After slavery during the 1860's this land was divided from the plantation and given to slaves but they had to divide and establish a system of their own. This is explained in the appendices how the community was developed.

On the east of the cemetery some of the early inhabitants of Garland are interred. History (by word of mouth states that this cemetery especially the upper portion east was the burial ground of native Indians who were in the area before Col. Johns Garland arrived. The Indians had been living around the Lon Creek Beds). Evidence of their living here is documented by artifacts found in the sand bed on the farm land. There are still arrowheads made from flat flint rock. The burial site in Garland is located between DeKalb, Texas and Oak Grove, Texas on a Farm Road.

It is said that this land was donated by a Garland and now has a sign title "Garland Cemetery." This sign was donated by one of the descendants of the fifth generation whose name is Roscoe Shavers. Laura Pearl Shavers 4th generation, attempted to outline the layout of the cemetery after the 1950's.

The cemetery of the white Garlands is located in Annona, Texas approximately 20 miles west of the Garland cemetery in Garland Community. Further information about Garland Community written by Laura P. Shavers Sands may be found in other areas of the book.

During slavery and shortly afterwards, slave masters and slaves were buried near or on the premises of their homes. After slavery a burial site was donated to former slaves in Garland.

Most of the white Garlands are buried in Annona including Col. John C. Garland and his wife Nancy.

The markers on the most important Garland graves are standing tall against the sun and sky. Some are reaching six or ten feet and signifying importance and wealth, a stark difference from the Negro or African American markers in Garland community. Only one or two stand more than three or four feet. Bannister Garland is one more than four feet.

See history of cemeteries written by Laura P. Shavers Sands.

Chapter 5

GARLAND NAMES FOUND IN the 1850 Census Index for Tennessee

in the Tennessee Archives Library, Nashville, TN

http://www.tngenweb.org/revwar/counties/davidson.htm
Tennessean in the Revolutionary War
ELISHA GARLAND 1835 Private, North Carolina Line, $74.00 Annual Allowance $222.00 Amount Received June 20 1833 Pension Started Age 72 (1835 TN Pension Roll)

http://genforum.genealogy.com/garland.html

Elisha and Lucy (Reives or Reeves) Garland had the following children:
Sally, born 1784;
Polly, born January, 1786;
Lucy, born February 1788;
Betsey, born January 31, 1790;
William, born May, 1792; Jesse , born May 26, 1794;
Kitty, born January, 1796;
Delilah, born March, 1798;
Patsey, born August 16, 1801; and
Orville Henderson, born about 1806.
This information came from Pension Claim Record No. W-926.

http://members.tripod.com/~PockyB/garland/2.html

Family Group Sheet
Father: Rev. Elisha Garland Born about 1788 in Carter County, Tennessee. Son of **Guthridge ("Old Gutch") Garland** and **Bridget Hampton.** Married 1809. Died 1875.
Mother: Nancy Roberson Born about 1793 in Virginia.
Children:
#1: Sarah ("Sallie") Garland Born about 1812. Married **Joseph Bowman.**
#2: Guthridge ("Captain Gutch") Garland Born 1814 or 1815. Married his first cousin, **Rebecca Garland,** daughter of **John William Thomas Garland** and **Rebecca Stanley.** Died 1896.
#3: Rev. Julius Samuel Garland Born about 1819. Married *1st* **Delitha Whitson.** Married *2nd* **Susannah -----.**
#4: Viann Garland Born 1822. Married **Aaron Burleson,** son of **Simeon Burleson** and **Mary ("Polly") Ledford.** Died 1876.
#5: Hampton Christenberry Garland Born 1825. Married **Jane Burleson,** daughter of **Simeon Burleson** and **Mary ("Polly") Ledford.** Died 1900.
#6: Nancy Garland Born about 1822. Married **Jonathan Burleson,** son of **Simeon Burleson** and **Mary ("Polly") Ledford.** Died 1903, Vian Valley, North Carolina.
#7: Locky C. Garland Born 1832. Married **William R. Stewart.** Died 1910.
#8: Thomas Garland Born 1838. Married **Patsy Slagle,** daughter of Jacob Slagle.
#9: John Calvin ("Cal") Garland Born 1841. Married **Martha Bailey, née Chandler,** widow of **Charles M. Bailey** and daughter of **Melchizedek Chandler**

Family Group Sheet
Father: Guthridge ("Old Gutch") Garland Born 1753 in Halifax County, North Carolina. Son of Married 21 September 1778 in Rowan County, North Carolina. Died 1848 Carter County, Tennessee. Buried
Mother: Bridget Hampton Born about 1760 in Halifax County, North Carolina. Daughter of **Ezekiel Hampton** and **Jane ("Jenny") Griggs.** Died Buried
Children:
#1: David Garland Born 20 July 1779 in Rowan County, North Carolina. Married *(his first cousin?)* **Sarah H. Garland,** daughter of **Humphrey Garland** and **Elizabeth Blankenship.** Died 24 April 1861 in Mitchell County, North Carolina.
#2: Jane ("Jenny") Garland Born 1780 [Some researchers say 1790] in Carter County, Tennessee. Married **Lazarus P. Phillips.** Died 1855 in Yancey County, North Carolina.
#3: Ezekiel Garland Born 1782 Carter County, Tennessee. Married, 30 March 1803, **Susannah Grindstaff,** daughter of **Nicholas Grindstaff.** Died about 1817.
#4: John William Thomas Garland Born 14 September 1783 or 1785 in Carter County, Tennessee. Married **Rebecca Stanley**, daughter of **Rickles Stanley** and **Olivia Howell** Died 24 October 1863.
#5: Rev. Elisha Garland Born about 1788 in Carter County, Tennessee. Married **Nancy Roberson.** Died 1875 in Mitchell County, North Carolina.
#6: Samuel Gutridge Garland Born about 1792 in Carter County, Tennessee. Married **Mary Alice ("Polly") Stanley,** daughter of **Rickles Stanley** and **Olivia Howell** Died 1883 in Fannin County, Georgia.
#7: Isabella Bridget Emma ("Bidda") Garland Born 1797 in Carter County, Tennessee. Married **Swinfield Stanley,** son of **Rickles Stanley** and **Olivia Howell** Died 1870.
#8: Nancy Delitha Garland Born 22 May 1798 in Carter County, Tennessee. Married **William Stanley,** son of **Rickles Stanley** and **Olivia Howell** Died 17 April 1881 in Fannin County, Georgia.
#9: Stephen Joseph Garland Born 13 April 1803 [Some researchers say 1793] in Carter County, Tennessee. Married *1st* **Elizabeth ("Betsy") McKinney,** daughter of **Samuel McKinney.** Married *2nd* **Elizabeth ("Betsy") Forbes,** daughter of **John Forbes** of Carter County, Tennessee. Died 6 July 1875.

Rb-1271-101
GARDNER, W. S. 31, Amanda 30, Virginia 4, Martha 3, Thomas 9/12, T Ky, We-11-690
GARDNER, William 33, Sarah M. 32, Catharine P. 9, William W. 5, Jane ZATLAND 22, T T, Wi-801-593
GARDNER, William 43, Rebecca 37, Elisabeth 18, Joseph 16, Thompson 14, Catharin 8, Milly 5, T NC, Wh-1564-228
GARDNER, William 25, Julia A. 24, James 1, T NC, Bl-835-823
GARDNER, Wm. 30, Mary 35, Henry 10, Andrew 8, Martha 6, John C. 4, Mary E. 2, Barcley R. 1, NC NC, Bo-736-104
GARDNER, Wm. A. 45, Martha G. 36, Wilkerson P. 18, James M. 14, Martha J. 12, William C. 9, Ester E. 2, T SC, Cr-739-110
GARDNER, W. B. 26, M. C. 21, Martin 2, Leonard 3/12, T T, Mt-322-311
GARDNER, Wm. H. 42, Harriet 24, James 18, John 16, Nancy 14, Louisa 12, Jacob 10, Mary 8, Margaret 6, Hester 4, Tomson 2, T T, Hu-775-293
GARDNER, William H. 43, Anny 40, William 21, Mary J. 18, John 17, Elender 16, Elizabeth 13, Jane 11, George W. 9, Disa 7, Charles 5, Thomas 3, Jesse 2, John R. 3/12, T T, Ro-1573-857
GARDNER, Wm. R. 21, Nancy 18, George S. 20, T T, Hu-128-202
GARDONSHIRE, Benjamin 36, Polina 35, James 10, Alto 9, Ares 5, Butler 3, Margaret 2, Lutecia GOODIN 13, T T, Ov-479-70
GARET, Archy M. 28, Sarah Ann 28, Martha 8, Elizabeth 8, Mary Ellen 5, Henry R. 3, William F. 1, T T, Fr-1005-149
GARETT, Stephen 27, Eliza 29, Hezekiah 4, Mary C. 3, Jno. S. 1/12, Jno BATY 58, Sarah FLOWERS 50, T T, Ms-904-180
GAREY, Nathan 51, Rebecca 46, George 18, John 15, Francis 13, Mary 9, William 7, Ephraim 5, Daniel 3, SC SC, D-206-563
GARGAES, Margaret 65, James 10, NC T, Mu-1481-693
GARGANIS, Benjamin 58, Nancy 40, Mary 15, Abram 11, Louisa 8, Pennina 4, Sarah 1, Jas. W. MASON 22, NC NC, G-636-336
GARGIS, A. 29, Mary 24, Martha 8, Louisana 4, T T, We-13-770
GARGIS, Ann 53, Peter WORKMAN 22, Nancy 31, George 3, Rosina 4/12, NC T, We-61-777
GARGIS, N. 35, Elizabeth 35, Mary 14, Susan 12, Sarah 10, Henry 7, Matilda 6, Franklin 3, Angeline 3/12, T NC, We-24-772
GARGUS, R. 30, Malaney 27, Andrew 4, Leander 2, Va T, We-16-771
GARL, John 18, John McCOY 24, T T, Je-974-792
GARLAND, Alphea 35, Mary 35, Jonathan 13, Elizabeth 11, Patsy 9, Tibitha 7, Mary 4, Levice 11/12, T T, Ct-89-457
GARLAND, Cemelia 39, Susan 16, Cemelia 14, Isabella 12, James 10, Louiza 8, T T, Wa-1179-368
GARLAND, David 24, Elizabeth 37, Nancy 10, Amy 8, James 5, Elizabeth 3, Celia 1/12, T NC, Ct-77-455
GARLAND, Eleanor 29, Mary M. 9, Sarah E. SIMPSON 15, Cornelius R. GARLAND 6, Ellen E. 5, T T, Wa-266-239
GARLAND, Elisha 26, Elizabeth 23, Jane 9, Joseph 7, Samuel 5, Wesley 3, William 3/12, Maryann STITT 14, NC NC, Mo-794-115
GARLAND, Hannah 26, Elizabeth C. 9, John 6, George W. 4, Kenedy 2, NC T, Ct-75-455
GARLAND, Isaac 43, Anna 31, Seraphina 10, Valentine 9, Ageline 7, Matilda 5, William H. 3, Harriet 7/12, Kenedy STOUT 21, T T, Ct-91-457
GARLAND, Jackson 21, Mary 17, T T, D-236-567
GARLAND, J. M. 30, Camilla F. 22, Samuel 3, Josephine 1, Ky T, Mt-506-338
GARLAND, Jessee 54, Jane 52, Orville H. 19, Francis M. 18, Jessee 16, Delila 13, James 10, Lucind 23, NC T, Wi-209-263
GARLAND, John 37, Nancy 35, Mary 16, Margaret 12, Joseph 10, Va NC, Mn-971-141
GARLAND, John G. 38, Susannah 37, Ezekiel 16, William W. 14, Sarah J. 12, Hannah 10, Elizabeth E. 6, John T. 3, Viney J. 10/12, T T, Ct-7-347
GARLAND, Joseph 63, Margaret 67, Eliza 28, T Va, Ha-192-28
GARLAND, Lewis 27, Rebecca 20, Nanay L. 3, Mahulda 1, T T, Cl-568-553
GARLAND, Mary E. 27, Nannie W. 9, Bettie H. 7, T T, Mt-141-285
GARLAND, Pryor 46, Margaret 37, Malinda 16, Isaac 15, Wiley 13, Samuel 9, Binnet 6, John 3, Elizabeth 2, T NC, Cl-675-571
GARLAND, Rebecca 25, Mary M. 9, Sarah 6, Martha 4, Bathena ODAM 60, T T, Ro-207-671
GARLAND, Sally 66, Delila 50, Thomas WILLIAMSON 27, T T, D-843-655
GARLAND, Samuel 50, Mary 31, Ulysses 13, Rebecca 12, Gerline 9, Jackson 7, Leonidas 3, Jamima WALDROP 62, Joseph GARLAND 20, T SC, D-1059-684
GARLAND, Sarah 35, Johnson 15, Alphia 7, NC T, Ct-66-454
GARLAND, Susannah 66, Mary 39, Samuel STREET 16, NC T, Ct-6-347
GARLAND, Tabitha 77, Elizabeth 32, Tabitha A. 11, Eliza J. HARRISON 23, NC T, Cl-676-571
GARLAND, Thos. L. 42, Sophronia R. 35, Martha A. E. 21, John C. 18, William W. 15, Isham G. 13, Thomas L. 11, Robert R. 9, Joseph D. 7, Sarah H. 5, Va NC, Ma-35-727
GARLAND, W. W. 38, Eliza 36, Minerva 8, Rebecca 6, Martha 3, Margaret 9/12, Va T, Ma-141-743
GARLAND, Wm. 45, Elizabeth 43, Thomas 20, Sarah MOORE 13, Joseph SCOTT 6, T NC, Wa-1140-362
GARLAND, William 33, Sarah 36, Pryor 12, Dilla 11, Andrew 9, Phebe 7, Nancy 5, William D. 1, Isaac 1/12, T T, Ct-92-458
GARLAND, William 66, Nancy 60, Mordica 25, William 19, Eliza J. 17, NC Va, Ct-79-456
GARLIND, Jno. 35, Salley 34, Nancy 16, David 11, Martha 8, Franklin 6, Jno. 5, Leanna 2, Fanny 11/12, T NC, Su-66-9
GARLINGTON, James 30, Mary J. 22, Nancy R. 3, Edith A. 1, NC T, Ma-831-548
GARMAN, George 46, Sally 50, Polly 30, Elizabeth 25, Rachel 22, Sally 18, George 19, Tiney 11, John 10, William 5, NC NC, Co-98-701
GARMAN, Isaac 35, Elizabeth 32, Polly Ann 13, Nancy 11, Maranda 9, Louisa 7, Lavany 5, John 2, NC T, A-644-91
GARMAN, Jacob 28, Margaret 30, Fine 9, Martha 7, Alphonse 5, Amelia S. 4, NC NC, Co-97-701
GARMAN, Sarah 50, Fanny J. 3, Drury E. S. 1, T T, K-1425-386
GARMAN, Susan 50, Elizabeth 21, Sally 19, Marcus 16, Wade 14, Polly 12, T T, Mn-1335-193
GARMAN, Alberry 45, Ruth 35, Alexander 18, Charlotte 14, Robert 12, Ruth A. 10, Artimissia J. 8, James 6, Isabella 4, William F. 1, T T, Cr-1647-248
GARMON, Robert P. 26, Joannah 28, Sarah J. 5, James R. 4, Easter M. 2, Roland 43, T T, Li-566-79
GARN, Preston 50, Mary 53, Louisa 15, Rebecca 13, Janet 17, Lafayett SMITH 25, Prucilla 21, Henry 4, Emoline 3/12, T T, H-87-749
GARNER, Alfred 21, Hannah 20, Melissa 1, T T, Hw-35-834
GARNER, Allen 59, Zelpha 38, Wm. 19, John 17, Allen 14, Dolly 13, T T, Bo-1456-201
GARNER, Amos 35, Nancy 37, Margaret 14, Rebecca 11, John 8, Polly 6, Dolly 3, Elizabeth 1, Emily 4/12, Jesse LYNCH 66, William 6, T T, Fr-1199-179
GARNER, B. 31, Joseph 12, Samuel 11, Richard 7, Ellen 5, T T, D-211-197
GARNER, B. C. 26, Charlotte 23, Wm. 3, Blakely 1, Charlotte COLEMAN 34, Susan 21, NC T, Hy-96-16
GARNER, Brice M. 26, Eliza J. 22, Louisa D. C. 1/12, T

Chapter 6

REUNIONS

The descendent of Ruth still gather together every two, three, or four years for a reunion. We meet to exchange experiences, to enjoy each other, to pass on the Garland legacy to small children, to eat, to ball back memories, to tell jokes, to meet the "new born," and to say a final good bye to those who have entered another realm. We welcome God's blessings and we are thankful for His love and mercy –Whomever we deem Him to be - as we worship and pray in a place of our choice.

Pictures of gatherings are offered in this book beginning in the late 1800s and some as late as 2007. The Garlands will continue to return to Garland to continue our quest for history of our loved ones and those who have gone on before.

Songs – 1996 Reunion

Garland-Shaver

<u>Tune of Freres Jacque</u>

We are family
We are family

Proud are we
Proud are we

Singing all together
Singing all together

Come and see
Come and see

We are family
We are family

Proud are we
Proud are we

Working all together
Working all together
Come and see
Come and see

Playing
Praying
Loving

Words by: M.S.J.

WE ARE HERE

WORDS & MUSIC BY
MATTIE S. JOHNSON

JUDY GREEN MUSIC Hollywood, CA 90028 (213) 466-2491 H-312

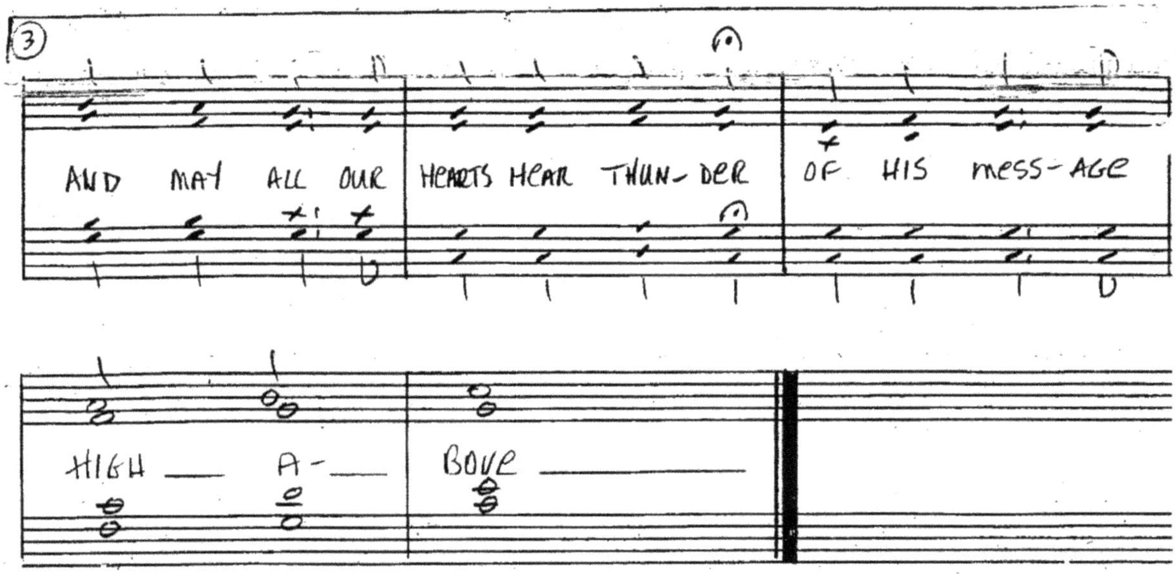

© COPYRIGHT 1993 BY MATTIE S JOHNSON
3511 GENEVA CIRCLE, NASHVILLE, TN, 37209

JUDY GREEN MUSIC Hollywood, CA 90028 (213) 466-2491 N-312

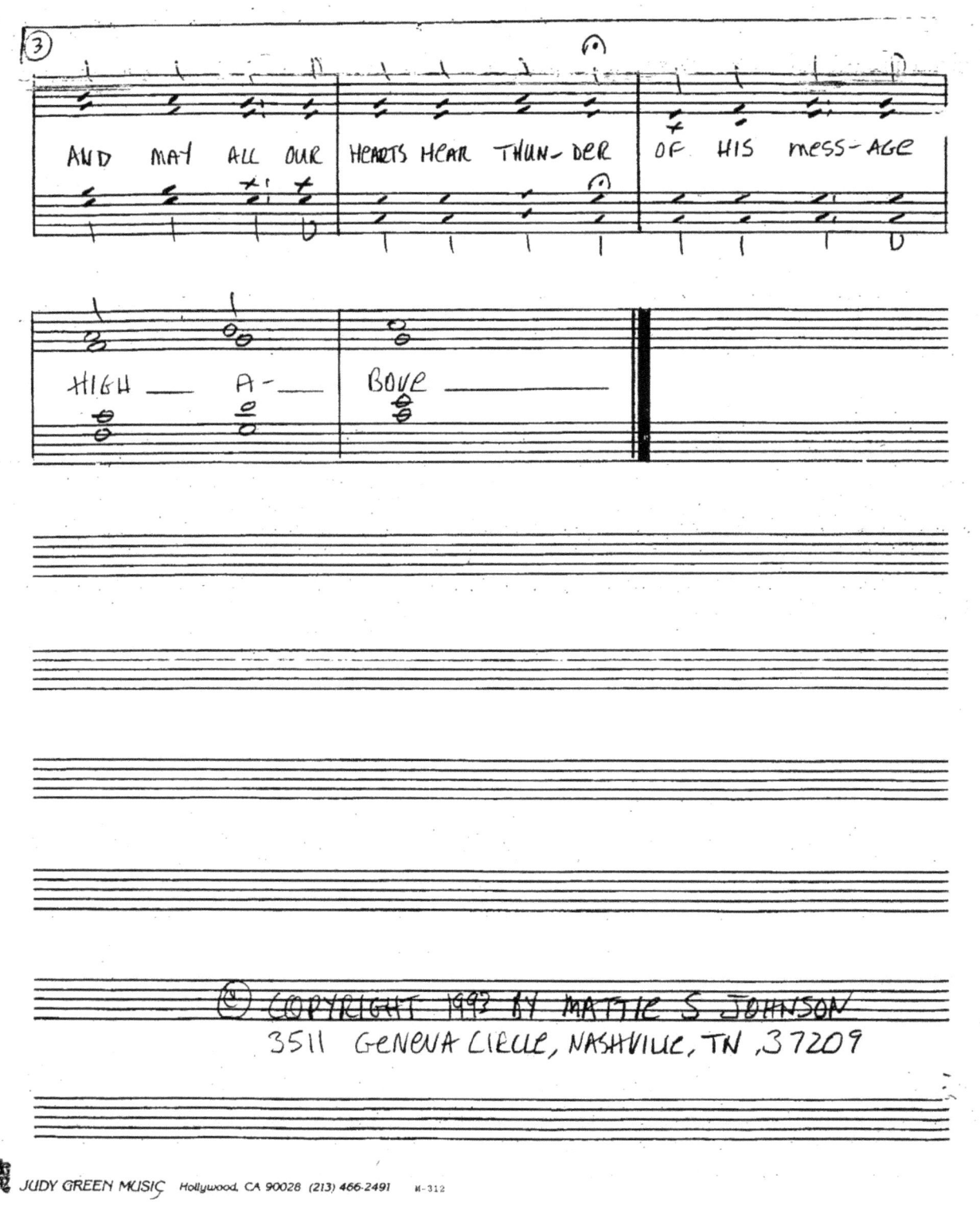

Garland-Shavers Family Reunion Song

Title: We Are Here

We are here to greet our brothers
We are here to see our sisters
We are here to sing all praises
For scattered relatives from all places.

We are here to love each other
Kiss the children and all mothers
Walk the places of our fathers
Sing the songs of God's good graces.

We are here for reminiscing
We are here for soul confessing
We are bringing all our children
To learn fast without mass guessing.

We are here to honor our parents
With a gift of old time sharing
Passing on to generations
All our borrowed goods and creations.

We are all our brother's keepers
We must work and not be weepers----sleepers
Striving daily to use our talents
Serving mankind and be valiant.
May God's blessings shine upon you
As you leave this place of wonder
Come again, and taste the sweetness
Of the fellowship and love.

And may all our hearts hear thunder,
Of His message high above.

(Ca) 1993 by Mattie S. Johnson

ODE TO RUTH

(Matrix of Garland Community)
Tune of: (For He's a Jolly Good Fellow)

Leader:	*There was a family called Garland* *Very large they say* *They wanted to find their family roots* *And searched hard in every way*
Audience:	*They searched hard in every way* *Searched hard in every way* *They wanted to find their family roots* *And they searched hard in every way*
Leader	*One day they found a maiden's name* *Who came from Tennessee* *Her father owned a plantation wide* *And kept her for posterity*
Audience	*Kept her for posterity* *Kept her for posterity* *Her father owned a plantation wide* *and kept her for posterity.*
Leader	*Her name was Ruth, her heritage* *Half Indian, half Caucasian proud* *Living content till a war of greed* *Tore families asunder indeed in crowds*
Audience:	*Tore families asunder in crowds* *Tore families asunder in crowds* *Living together till a war of greed* *Tore families asunder in crowds*
Leader:	*She was given to his humble slave* *Jim was his name* *They raised a family of their own* *And this is your Heritage*
Audience:	*And this is your Heritage* *And this is your Heritage* *They lived together in marriage*

And this is your Heritage

Leader

They had ten children of their own
One of them named James
James Polk is your grandfather
Jennie his mate all claim

Audience:

Jennie Knight his mate all claim
Jennie Knight him mate all claimed
James Polk is your grandfather
Jennie Knight his mate all claim

Leader

So be ye all comforted
If you are a descendant of James
Or one of James's sisters or brothers
Any one of Ruth's clans your name

Audience

Any one of Ruth's clans your name
Any one of Ruth's clans your name
Any one of James' sisters or brothers
Any one of Ruth's clans your name
Any one in Ruth gag is your name.

MILLENNIUM CAPSULE CELEBRATION

Dedicated To

The Memory of Our Forefathers

James Polk Garland & Iverson E. Shavers

November 2000

Garland Community

DeKalb, TX

PROGRAM

Prayer: Lord's Prayer or Individual Quietness

Greetings: Iverson E. Shavers

Reunion Song: We are Here The People

Responsive Reading:

Leader: *We are God's Creation and His gift to this universe. We come this day to give thanks to a power greater than ourselves, for allowing us to witness the dawning of a brand new millennium. It is a day that most of us never dreamed of seeing. For this reason we make the following pledge.*

Leader: *We pledge to honor our maker, our parents, ancestors, teachers, ministers and others who have made a difference in our lives.*

People: *We so pledge!*

Leader: *We pledge to return to our roots whenever possible to make connection with the spirit of our ancestors, and to honor their teachings and principles.*

People: *We so pledge!*

Leader: *We pledge to use our God given talents and gifts to advance the cause of love, growth and service and to help make the world a better place for others after we leave it.*

People: *We so pledge!*

Leader: *We pledge to take advantage of our educational and religious systems to help and keep our hearts in tune with the spirit of love and to be productive and giving citizens – realizing that the only way to have life to its fullest is to give it away – in talent, deeds or other forms of giving and serving.*

People: *We so pledge!*

Leader: *We now deposit our memories, our gifts and talents in appreciation of our loved ones in the Capsule to be opened 50-100 years from this date November 2000 to remind others who come after us that our gifts of time came from the Almighty power whomever we perceived Him to be.*

Prayer: *Almighty God – we deposit these gifts from you for safe keeping in memory of your great love and sacrifice. Amen*

Leader: *Closure of gifts.*

Release of balloons.

NOTE: *If there is something in the program that you are not in accord, please just stand and commune with yourself and nature. (Thank you for coming to this dedication).*

The Tennessee Garland and Albert King Family (?late 1800's: The couple seated n the left are Albert King (incidentally, brother of Mattie Johnson Savers, Grandfather Robert's mother) and Tennessee Garland King, Sister of James Polk Garland (see Albert King in the family of Owen and Julie Shavers, 1870 Census). The woman to the right of Tennessee is her mother, Ruth Garland, Grandmother Laura's paternal grandmother.

Henry Scott Family (?1860-80):

The woman seated is Victoria (Hunter ?) Scott, mother of Jennie and grandmother of Laura Garland Shavers -- Standing are Sally Scott, Clinton Scott, and Earnest Scott (It is unclear if these were her children).

James Polk Garland Family (?late 1800's): The picture was in poor condition. The couple standing to the right is James Polk Garland and his second wife, Millie Garland. On the far left is James Polk's brother Hartwell Garland, The girl standing in the front is Zetha Garland (later Webb), daughter of Hartwell Garland, next to her Porter and Sanders Eastland and standing behind Porter is Millie Eastland. The Eastland children were Millie's children by her first marriage. The young man to the left of Hartwell is unidentified.

<u>1914 Family Reunion:</u> Standing from the right, Owen Shavers (wife, Charity Johnson Shavers is torn from the picture), his sister, Janie Shavers Forte (?), Mattie Johnson Shavers, her husband, Iverson Shavers, William Shavers, his wife, Effie Garland Shavers, Clayton Bell, his wife Ethel Shavers Bell, Alma Henix, Robert and Laura Shavers (holding daughter Laura Pearl). First row from right, Charlie Johnson, Hattie Shavers Henix (seated), Major Shavers (kneeling, son of William, Sr.), behind him his brother Robert Shavers and William Shavers, Jr., then Lorenzo, Helen and Fred Shavers

1983

YALE

Early Garland Settlers, Ruth Garland, front row right

L to R. Robert, Minnie, William, & Hattie Shavers Year?

Harry Shavers is standing next to the girl 1910?

Grandpa Polk (tallest) & Grandma Mattie

Chapter 7

Other Inspirational and Influential Individuals Who May Have Had an Impact on the History of Garland Community Inhabitants

HELEN BERNICE 4TH GENERATION

The oldest daughter of Laura Garland Shavers and Robert Shavers

Helen (sister) gave the oration for her class at graduation time. Her subject was: "She Stand at the Bar of Justice" (author: Paul L. Dunbar).

She was the valedictorian of her class. She spent a short time in Bishop College and then married Ennis Jackson from New Boston, Texas. To that marriage they were blessed with twins: Walter Curtis and Robert Ertist and Wilma Jean. Sister as we called her was one of the best culinary artist I have even known. As I was told by my oldest siblings, she started cooking at five years old. My mother was "in the family way" as they say so often she could not care for the younger ones and "Sister" had to take over. She was like a second mother.

JANE GARLAND WALLER

Jane Garland, my grandfather's sister, came by our home often to visit Mama. She never stayed very long. It was as though she was passing by on her way to her h ome. I remember once when she was passing through, by the time she arrived she had run out of snuff brushes. She would ask Millie and me to go and find a black gum bush and break off the new born branch so that she could crush the end to make a brush to dip her snuff. We would gladly do her bidding because she always had a goodie for us and would talk to us about what we would be when we grew up. We thought she was a fortune teller and could see the future. She told me that I would be a traveler and would travel far and wide.

Sarah Garland

Aunt Sarah, another sister of James Polk, lived in a small but behind Cousin Jessie's house. When I was growing up, we thought she was like a hermit. We very seldom saw her. She never came by and we often wondered why she had the kind of isolated lifestyle that we witnessed.

Robert Garland

Robert Garland was an educator who had learned to read and write at his mother's knee. He had no formal education but knew more about education than his other sisters and brothers and was one of the first teachers in Garland Community. His picture hangs in the corridor of the school. I saw it each day as I entered the door and felt proud that he was a relative who had helped to establish a learning environment other than at home and church. He is deemed to be a great pioneer in education at Garland. Others followed: a Mr. Winston who was white, also I don't remember except for Professor Major Johnson who taught my mother, and Professor U.S. McClellan who taught me.

<u>The Tennessee Garland and Albert King Fame (?late 1800's:</u> The couple seated on the left are Albert King (incidentally, brother of Mattie Johnson Shavers, Grandfather Robert's mother) and Tennessee Garland was the sister of James Polk Garland. (see Albert King in the family of Owen and Julie, 1870 Census). The woman to the right of Tennessee is her mother, Ruth Garland, Grandmother Laura's parental grandmother.

L to R. Robert, Minnie, William, & Hattie Shavers Year?

Harry Shavers is standing next to the girl 1910?

Grandpa Polk (tallest) & Grandma Mattie

James Polk Garland

My grandfather, James Polk Garland, (Ruth's son) appeared to be a revered gentlemen of his time. He was "well off," and had a nice home. At three years old, I could not see all of him. He appeared to be seven feet tall and I was looking up to see all of him forever it seemed. He was a former business man who had tenants living on his farm. The person living in his home was called Daisy; his half-brother or other such relative could not care for her and sent her to live in a relative's home. At that time another mouth to feed was unbearable or tenuous so he or she had to be willing to work as a tenant if they were homeless. When my mother and father married, their family grew very fast. There were very few conveniences; there was not running water in the home. If the well (a wood lined structure) fell in, water had to be carried to the house by pail for cooking or washing.

On one particular day, my mother had gone to the spring to fetch water; my grandfather understood her plight and came by to check on her, as he often did. When we looked up, there he stood with his khaki pants, a colored shirt and a Stetson hat watching us play in the sand. When he asked, "Where is your mama?" we happily told him that we were not allowed to talk to strangers, but to him we said, "down to the spring."

Daisy

Jack Garland was a half-brother of James Polk who lived in the Marshall, Texas area after slavery. He did not live in DeKalb. The story told was that a minister came to DeKalb and talked to Grandpa about the hardships of where he was and his predicament. Uncle Jack had many children, one of them was named Daisy. Grandpa Polk agreed to take Daisy to his house to help him. That is how Daisy came to live with Grandpa. Daisy was really a member of the Garland Family, Jack Garland's daughter, I am told.

Smithie Garland Hubbard –Age?

Laura Garland Shavers –Age?

James Garland

Aunt Effie Garland Daughter of James Polk Garland

Aunt Effie Garland was a very quiet and undisturbed person. Her gardens were always green and producing fresh and abundant fruit and vegetables to share with others. Some people often wondered what her secret was. I suspect it was love and constant care.

Aunt Effie must have had an excellent memory. The poem below was recited many times during her school years. It is recorded here by her sister Laura Garland Shavers, the author is unknown.

Aunt Effie and Uncle William, my father's brother were the parents of four children, namely Ulysses, Harry, Theopholis (Teet), a girl who deceased early in life and Robert (Bob).

Note

The Holts and the Kings from Tennessee married into the Garland family. (Ruth's and James (Jim) Garland.

Some of the descendants of the King family (Albert King and Tennessee Garland King) still live in Garland Community. Especially the descendants of the Betts. Children of Opra Tel still live there.

Third Generation

Uncle Jim and Zilpha Garland

We were not allowed to slip across the field to go through Uncle Jim's yard which was across the fence from Grandpa Polk's house but sometimes the temptation was too great especially when the peaches were ripe—he had the most beautiful large plums one could ever imagine hanging on his trees. Most times when we were caught we were scold but the scolding could never be as strong as we needed. But, oh the joy of one sweet plum! The memory is still salivating.

Effie Shavers

Effie Garland Shavers and Uncle William

When I was a small child we (my family) visited my Uncle and Aunt Effie during the summer. They lived near Red River nearly 10-15 miles away. We had to leave DeKalb (Garland) before sun-up to arrive at Aunt Effie's house by 10 o'clock because travel by wagon was very slow. We had to get permission to pass through the penitentiary grounds and over the bayou through open prairie where buffalo roamed and we had to be very quiet not to disturb the buffalo. We didn't want to start a stampede. I was always afraid but we always made the trip successfully. What an adventure. Later when we were older we were fortunate enough to visit our older sister Helen, in Hot Springs, Arkansas about 125-150 miles from DeKalb, Texas riding in a car (a Ford or Chevrolet) with windows down and reading the signs. These signs were usually about "Burma Shove." To us this was "advanced education on cloud nine."

U.S.

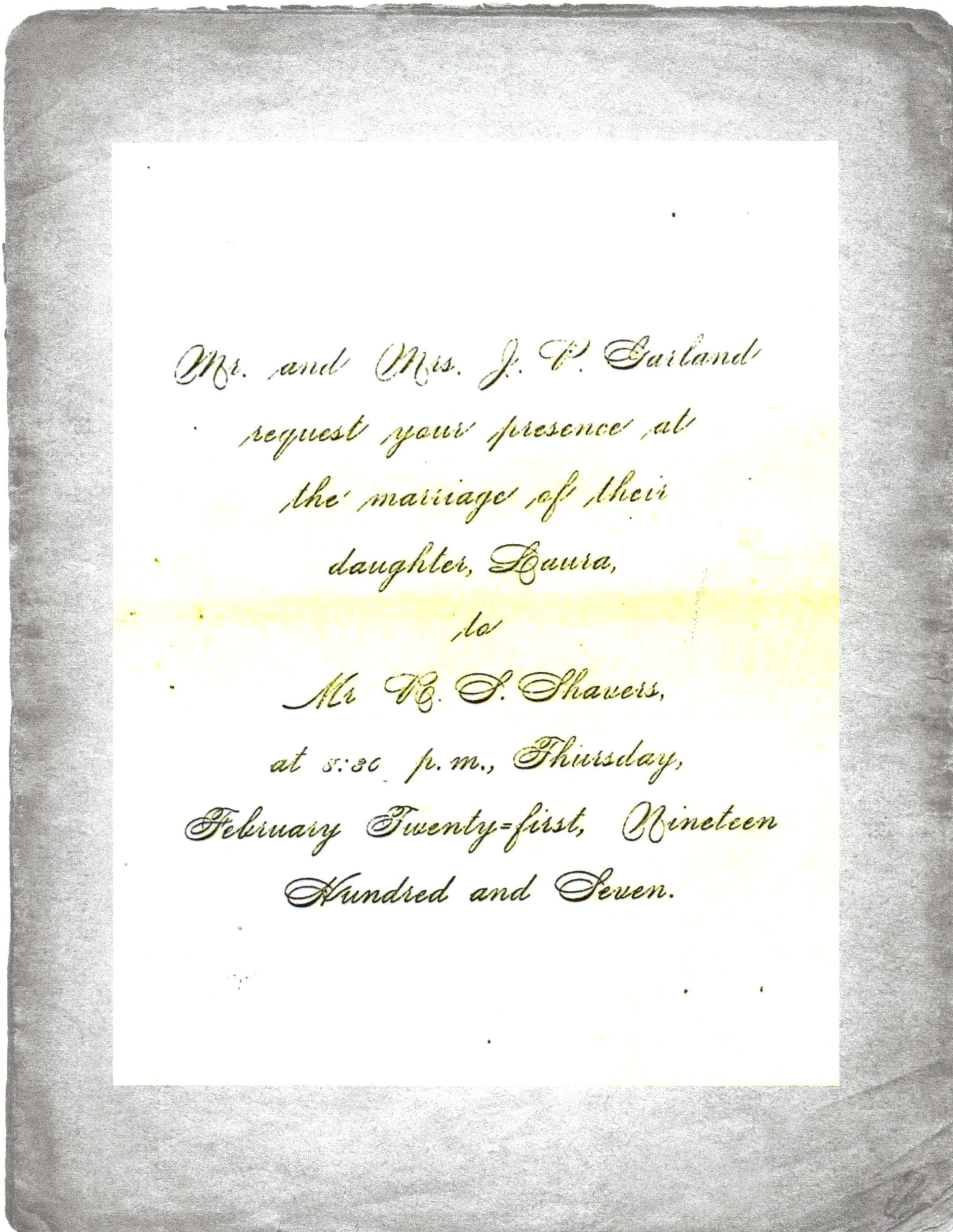
Mr. and Mrs. J. P. Garland
request your presence at
the marriage of their
daughter, Laura,
to
Mr R. S. Shavers,
at 5:30 p.m., Thursday,
February Twenty-first, Nineteen
Hundred and Seven.

In Memoriam

Of the Late

Robert Stanley Shavers

•

•

Abide With Me

2:00 P.M.
SUNDAY, NOVEMBER 22, 1959
MT. PISGAH BAPTIST CHURCH

Smithie Garland Hubbard

Auntie Smithie, Uncle john Hubbard, momma's sister lived in Hooks, Texas about 25 miles east of DeKalb, Texas. Uncle John and Aunt Smithie were the parents of six children. Millie and I visited many summers with them. Many times fussing and fighting but we loved each other especially Love (Geneoa) and Norman. My favorite cousin in this family was Gus Hubbard. He was a loving and caring person. Once during WWII while working at an ammunition depot I was not able to get home to DeKalb, Texas. When night came there was no place for me to go. He saw me and asked how I was going to get home. I told him I had no way to get home, buses were not running that late. He said, "come on with me." He placed me in the bed of his truck and covered me with a blanket and coat and came through-out the night to check on me. Whenever I think of such a deep and compassionate love, my heart skips a beat and the tears start to flow. Thanks to God for sending a soul like this to rescue me. He must have been an angel. He was kind to everyone. The people in his neighborhood must have thought so also. A road has been named in his honor in Hooks, Texas.

The Children of Robert and Laura Shavers
50th Anniversary

Sister Helen's twin boys and sister Wilma Jean with dog
Two boys with witheir grandfather Walter Jackson and Robert E. Jackson

Chapter 8

POETRY

••••••••••

HERITAGE

Family! You are a part of the ocean that flows
And the mountains that rise us
from the belly of the sea.
And leaves that drift
from the blowing wind.

You are the fire that burns
in souls of many
You relate to the robin's wing and song
On each wing you carry a message
Of all things wrought
by the angels singing
You are a part of creation's mold
Your souls runs deep among the silent.
All particles within the dungeon deep
Swirl forever in your being.
You are here under a giant's feet
Who walks your dreams of tomorrow
you may stand on His shoulder
I repeat:
Your dwelling in His promise
to seek and keep.

From Eternity Rising by Mattie S. Johnson
Page 26, salutation changed to Family

Written for the Women's Group of St. Andrews Presbyterian Church (USA)

CHANGE

A Poem by Mattie S. Johnson

We arise each day to begin again
Renewing our thoughts and adjusting within
With visions and dreams and relations and schemes
But the revolution of time takes its toll therein.

With truth and faith in God, we are born again in love
We, like flowers spring forth and prove
That seeds planted in rich soil prosper and rise
Bringing joy to others within compromise.

Tho' pressed by every for and fear
We will not shirk our duty though we sometimes tear.

We renew our spirit through Jesus Christ
And will revive in others there potential through our sacrifice

In this world of technology, permissiveness greed and crime
Children cry out, rebel, and need us most of the time
Let us work diligently to nurture, listen and hear them.
Through the power of Christ and love given us,
We can take time to heal, restore and renew them.

The tools we use for brow-beating others
Into joining us in our vices
Pay meager dividends in a crisis.
We can give up our pride and renew our souls,
By investing in our treasures;
Our children and youth of today and their goals.

We, as women, must take the lead
To create change in every nook and corner;
Every spectrum of our civil and spiritual systems to succeed.
We must stop the world epidemics of sordid diseases
And experimenting with the bizarre;
There is an order of God's universe of love, joy, and power;
If we would only look—it is clear
To effect change we must listen to His Word without fear
Every second of the day, every minute—every hour.

DON'T YOU BELIEVE FAT MEAT'S GREASY?

(This actually occurred once when my grandfather reprimanded my uncle)

Boy!
Don't you believe fat meat's greasy?
"Yes sir Papa, yes sir Papa!"
Pull down your pants
and bare to the breezes!

This one's for my last
Promise – *Wam!*
This one's for months passed – *Wam!*

This one's for sassing
and talking back to us *Wam*!
I lay this one on for
the lies and the cuss – *Wam!*

Now don't you believe
fat meat's greasy?

"Yes sir Papa! Yes sir Papa!

MEMORY QUOTATIONS FROM HER SISTER EFFIE

Written by my mother (Laura Garland Shavers)
author unknown

The apple bough half hid the house
where live a lonely widow,
Behind there stood the chestnut wood
before it spread the meadow.

She had no money in her till
she was too poor to borrow,
With her lame legs she could not beg
for no one shared her sorrow.

She had no wood to cook her food
and but one chair to sit in,
Last spring she lost a cow that cost
a whole year's steady worn knitting.

She had worn her fingers to the bone
her back was growing double,
One day the pig tore up her wig
but that's not half her trouble.

Her best black gown had faded brown
her shoes were all in tatters,
She had no pair for Sunday wear
said she, "It little matters."

"Nobody ask me now to ride
my garments are not fittin',
And with my crutch I cannot much
but hobble off to meet."

"I still reserve my testament
although the acts are missing,
And Luke is worn and Hebrew torn
on Sunday 'tis a blessing."

"And other days I open
before me on the table,
And there I sit and read and knit
as long as I am able."

One evening she had closed her book
but still she sat there knitting,
Mew the cat upon the mat
"Mew, mew," the spotted kitten.

"I was dark but hark, bow wow the bark
of Ranger at the wicket,
"Is Ranger barking at the moon
Or what can be the matter?"

"But hard what's that?"
She hears the old gate latches
"Is it the wind that banks the gate,
And I must knit my stocking?"

"But hush dear me what can it be?
For that's someone knocking.
Dear me, dear me, who can it be?
Where is my crutch and handle?
Where's that match? And haste the scratch!"
She cannot light the candle.

Blue burns the match, the tinted match
and then the candle glistens,
Along the floor beside the door
the cold white moonlight shimmers.

"Rat-tat-tat, scratch," Up flies the latch!
"Good evening, Mrs. Warner."
The kitten spits and lifts his back,
his eyes fell on the stranger.

The old cat's tail roughed big and black,
loud barked the old dog Ranger.
"Sit down," the widow gives a chair
"Get out!" she says to Rover.

"Alas, I do not know your name."
"No matter," says the stranger.
"My way is lost and with the frost
I feel my fingers tingle."

And on his back, he wears a sack
his staff was stout and heavy.
"I feel a heart beat fast with fear
but what can be the danger?"

"Can I do aught for you kind sir?"
"I am hungry," said the stranger.
"I have no food for you or me
for boiling or for baking."

"I've food for you, for you and me,"
and gave his sack a shaking.
Out rattled knives and forks and spoons
and eggs, potatoes plenty.

One large soup dish
two plates of fish
and bread enough for twenty.
(missing 3 verses)

And Rachel, calming her surprise as well as she was able
And following this two bowls of fish
a tea urn on the table.

Strange, was it not?
Each dish was hot
but not a plate was broken,
The cloth was laid and all arranged
before a word was spoken
.
"Sit up! Sit up! And we will sup
Dear Madam while we are able,
For low the room is poor and small
for such a farmer's table."

CROSS THE CREEK

Cross the creek
To enter the field
Cross the creek
To return for a meal
Cross the creek
If forgotten special hoe
Cross the creek
To work some more
Stay the feet
To hug the log
Stay the feet
As a grasping frog
Don't look down
If water is deep
Straddle and inch
Your way to seek
Night is falling
Try not to fail
Vermin are watching
To catch at will
Cross the creek
And head toward home
Drop the hoe
And leave it alone
Cross the creek
And hurry home
Supper is waiting
fear not or roam
Wade the creek
To wash the feet
No mud allowed.
At the door to keep
Work is limited
To field and plow
Work for yourself
or by the hour

UNDERNEATH THE WILLOW

She was under the willow
reading a book
branches weeping
over her private nook.

A spring barrel
close by
for a cool sip in shade.
A soul-mate stood watching,
for intruders not bade.

Lon Creek flowed ambly by
with a quiet ripple,
music to the ear
While knowledge was gained
by the same gripper.

No one ever found
the hide-out in secret
Only two knew
but now memory will
keep it.

THE "DOODLE BUG" DOWN THE LANE

Down the lane
we played in the sand
among the beetles and ants.

The more we played
the more they ran.

We tried to call
them back by name
to claim their home
though not the same.

Their Song
"Doodle Bug"
"Doodle Bug"
Come to the top
Your house is tumbling down!

THE COWS ARE OUT

Who's here to mend the fences?
They're all scattered here and about
To herd them in a matter for doubt
The cows are out!

Call Lee or Max to gather them together
while I dig with post hole and count
the footage for wire to stretch farther.
The cows are out!

HITCHING WAGONS 1900'S

Every man-child was skilled in the art of hitching a team
Placing the bridle on horse or mule
Bit in mouth, working back and forth

Proper placement of the strap
Behind the ears
Locking in the gears
To the traces and the single tree
Always properly

Ready to take the team to town
Sometimes this took hours
Though scarcely found
But necessarily had to be
To start another week properly

Though years have passed
And the "nuke" arrived
It is still important and wise
To hitch our wagons to a team
And await the ending through
Time and a dream.

OPEN THE GATE

I hear the hooves
And the buggy wheel
Rutting the road as they move
Open the gate

Open the gate
The sound of the whip
You can never forget
Run to meet him before its too late
To a-lights, his steed before Sunset

Open the gate
With a firm grip
Tomorrow is a-coming
With sunlight over flowing
And hope in it Open the gate

MY JOURNEY

When I have burned
the last atom of my soul
may it generate
enough energy
to form a star.

You asked
where do you fit
in the galaxy
of stars
one atom to another?

I say to you
when the stars
with the sun burn
with evolution
I will be there.

I'll be there
advancing
toward you
but challenging
all the laws of earth
and the universe.

For you and I
were meant to be, reaching out
for unity
and meaning
of a force that drew us together
in this world
of life in
the cosmos.

When every simple
element
blown by the wind
for life's needs
is present
I'll be there.

I'll be there
across time and space
on a journey
of particles
and matter
ever changing
to infinity
through
natures order.

Inspired by Journey Into One; The Final Unity. By Peter Mikkelsen
Poem by Mattie S. Johnson

SONGS OF THE SHIFTING SAND

Like shifting sand
That rolls and breaks with the wind
To form a new pendage
Again
With music chilling the air in every
Chism in the land
And a resonance that
Pierces the soul
And
As angels in heaven become enthralled
I have seen and heard the gathering of each grain
Moving the earth beyond
Its fold
And be buried as they
Are lain Covered by tears of rain
At the foot of pyramids
Lending shadows
Measured by their worth again

Mattie Shavers Johnson

BEGINNINGS

From the beginning of beginnings
One man kissed the earth and then
Molded with hand the future
of things to come, and wiped out sin.

One man can start the wheels of tomorrow
And lighten the load of weighted men
Give rise to a bleeding heart in sorrow
Feed one child; fill multitudes within.

Love one moment without fear or reprisal
Fight one battle for eternal victory, and when
Honor comes, face it, and discover the miracle
of rewards that come to those who win

One man can dream one dream to exercise
his longing
Pray one prayer for believers, lost and helpless
Walk one mile for freedom—marchers, singing
Longing to appease a hurt, with happiness.

On goes the stream of drops of beginnings
Leading to oceans that control our land
Each man carrying the sum of his winnings
In depths of his ocean from deeds to man.

SONG

By: Charles W. Johnson

A setting sun heralds the beginnings on
something new—an awakening

The accumulating dark and dusk of the night
covers the shadows of the day.

Misdirected hopes and unexpected frustrations
are laid to rest with yesterday.

Yet these things make a sound assumed by
all of nature's features and some of its
creatures of life and the night.

In a gathering of the gloom, the crickets
chirp a refrain of identifiable existence,
followed soon by the plea of the chee-chee
bird that he too be heard

The croak of the isolated frog compliments
this symphony of nature.

Roaring to a frenzy with the crescendo of
the winds and descending to the levels of
the whispering breeze, the amphitheater is
lighted by the twinkling stars.

Softly the music of the troubled soul
asserts itself as the master of all in the
loneliness of the night . . .

The dawn and fortissimo

And with the blasting of the sun on its
announcement of a new day, yesterday's
sorrows and last night's mysteries are
blended together in a rhapsody for now. . .

In this Song.

It's significance: The beginning of a people, a new day.

PHOTO GALLERY

Alvin and Millie Shavers Collins Family

Top row: Alvin, holding Tieri J., Millie, Alvin's wife, Sherry, Millicent, Joyce Collins Caldwell

Bottom row: Tanya; Dona: Phyllis, Joyce's daughter and James Inverson

Tanya Duncanson Family Pictures
Descendants of Millie O. Shavers Collins

Tanya Duncanson & Daughter Tanya, Jemila Duncanson

Tanya Duncanson and husband, Michael

Top Picture: Sherry Williams, daughter of Millie Collins with grandchildren, Talitha and Esteban

Bottom Picture: Sherry Williams with son Ronald and wife, Grace and grand - daughter, Talitha

Dr. Iverson Charles Bell

October 12, 1916 - May 22, 1984

ARMY

REFERENCES

1. The files of Robert S.1 and Laura Shavers
2. The Unpublished work of Ethel Garland McPeters
3. The collected files of Laura Pearl Shavers Sands and Millie O. Shavers Collins
4. Word of mouth, Lorenzo B. Shavers, Jr., and Barbara Ann Shavers
5. Photographs of the Garland Shavers family Reunions
6. Bowie County Court House archives, New Boston, TX
7. Red River County Court House archives, Clarksville, TX
8. Miller County Public Library archives, Texarkana, TX
9. Madison County Court House archives, Jackson, TN
10. Davidson County archives, Nashville, TN
11. Wilson County Telephone Directory, Lebanon, TN
12. Newspaper articles, Texarkana, TX
13. Tourism Guide – East Texas, 2000
14. Grave markings, Annona, TX

From the Archives of the State of Tennessee, Nashville, TN
Geological Research by Mrs. White, a staff member at Meharry Medical College
Genealogical Search Bowie County Archives, New Boston, TX
The files of Ethel Garland McPeters
Newspaper Clippings, DeKalb, TX
Word of Mouth History by Descendants of Ruth Garland
Research and Files of Raynard Kington
The files of Laura Pearl Shavers Sands
Computer and Geological Search by Livette S. Johnson
The Files of Millie Collins, DeKalb, TX
Geological Search of Raynard Kington
Geological Search in Clarksville, TX
Archives (Court Houses)
Archives in Library at Texarkana, TX
Geological Search in Court House, Madison County, TN (Jackson, TN)
Research by Stanley and Agnes Shavers
Google Geological Search
Garlands and Shavers by Iverson and Jenna Benton
History of Bowie County
Supplement to Bowie County
Citizens Tribune, Sunday, July 18, 1993
Submitted by Jo Lyon Audrey

Read: Brochure of Activities from Garland – Shavers Reunion distributed unpublished work by descendants of Ruth Garland 1993-2010

Read: Landon Garland Papers, Vanderbilt University Archives
Read: Deed to J. D. Garland to J. D. Calhoun
Archives at Col. 14, page 404 New Boston Court House, New Boston, TX
The Bowie County Citizens Tribune, DeKalb News
129 E. N. Front Street, New Boston, TX 75570 (903-628-5801)

Descendants of Slaves now Pillars of Community History of Bowie County

Supplement to Bowie County Citizens Tribune, Sunday, July 18, 1993
By: used by permission Jo Lynn Autrey

PROLOGUE

I had experienced segregation but not rationalized this phenomenon. It never occurred to me until my college years, that identity can play a major role in how one thinks of him or herself and how we as people think of each other. Society has tagged groups ethnic or certain population as “less than” if that group or population or more than even individual does not meet or conform to a certain standard or cannot prove his or her identity as one of this or that, Everyone has to carry a card to be eligible for this or that to obtain status, money, food, shelter, clothing or any type of service to exist; to be a part of this universe.

This phenomenon has been practiced or promoted since biblical times; one is or was a member of the descendants of Abraham; or maybe from one of the tribes of Israel; hence and to the same extent we are still practicing from Africa to Texas to the extent of the entire genre to exist one must belong to a family, group or population and it is suggested that one must believe in or belong to a church or choices; To have belief in and have faith in a Power greater than self or invent, create or borrow one; consequently, we are forever searching, digging, proving, studying and looking for our roots to become whole and contributing, serving and loving each other, in spirit and in joy/truth.

APPRECIATIONS

My deepest appreciation is extended to:

- My brother Iverson (Honey) for sharing his memories and experiences of growing up and of the people and relatives in the Community (Garland) he remembered;
- To my sister, Laura Pearl, for keeping our family history safe after Mama and Dad died. Thank you for doing everything for us when we were growing up; I don't think we could have de it without you!
- To Jenna for her love of family so demonstrated in her retrieving, storing, and recording of information about the family as obtained from my mother's father's files kept by Laura Pearl an for the many mailings she sent me;
- To Myrtle for her support and companionship;
- To Mildred and her children, especially her son Raynard, who took their love and spread the history that they gathered from researching, and who placed the Community on the National Register of Historic Places;
- To my son Charles (Skipper) who volunteered to drive me to Texas, taking me through many towns, stopping and researching to gather information about the migration of Col. John Garland and his family to DeKalb, TX. This was a journey which took us to the archives, county courthouses, and libraries in Madison County, Texarkana, New Boston, DeKalb, Anona, and Clarksville.
- To Bessie Merle for her serious efforts in writing about her connection;
- To Thelma Ray for her contributions in refreshing my memory about her family connections;
- To Mrs. Hall for her patience, support and efforts in bringing this project to completion;
- To my daughter, Livette, who loved to play and learn on the computer and to trace "roots," thank you for your research and for all your love;
- To my son Phillip, who is always there for me, finding time to take care of every logistical need I have, and to him and his children for their love and belief in me;
- To Stanley for his search concerning the History of Education before and after slavery in the United States;

- To Lorenzo (Pete) and Denise for their love, ever ready and available to support me any way possible;

- To the memory of my twin, Millie O. and her children who remembered as much or more than I could ever recall, and also to Mille for her collaborative work with me in 1993 in organizing the format for our future family reunions;

- To Mrs. White, a colleague, who while volunteering at Meharry Medical College, did some research and found Garlands in many states in the United States and abroad;

- To Gus Hubbard, (deceased), who did not help to write this book but played a significant role in being my protector during WWII while working at an ammunition plant, who covered me in a truck bed for the night when I had no other place to go;

- Also to James Germany who walked me home from the dark road when there was not one else around;

- To. N. A. Eastland who drove me home so often during war time;

- To my brother, Fred, who always looked after me;

- To my brother, James, (Jim) who took me to all of the games and social events available to us in the area;

- To my oldest brother, Lorenzo for his love and concern;

- To my oldest sister Helen, who was like a mother to me;

- Mable Garland for her love;

- To Juanita Garland for her love of community and family;

- To my teachers, ministers and other members in the community. Thank you, all!

- To my cousin Geneva (Love) Hubbard, my play mate and friend with whom Millie and I visited so many summers;

- To Emma Wisdom for her constant support;

- To Saint Andrew's Presbyterian Church for their constant prayers and concerns;
- To Berma Lee Garland, my playmate, for many wonderful memories;
- To Herman and Hazel Robinson for their love and just for being;
- To Wendy, my Godchild, for her love and support and for offering to type and help edit this book;
- And especially to my husband, Charles, my life and everlasting love;
- I wish I could remember all of my loved ones who have loved and supported me throughout the years;
- To the McDaniels and Johnson families for their love and support;
- To Tonya Collins Ducanson for final assistance in completing this book.

To all other family members who would like to have participated, but did not have the time or could not for reasons unknown;

Thank you

Most of all -- to God Be Praised!

My heart pangs when I think of all the work (a labor of love) done by Wendy and Shae to bring this book to fruition and all of the time and work done by Barbara Ann, Dawn Gloria, Ted and Carmen, Pete, Glenn and Shelecia to celebrate the birthday of Clarice and all others I can't recall, especially Thelma ray for time and pictures.

APPENDIX

INFORMATION ABOUT SOME OF RUTH'S CHILDREN IN THEIR OWN HAND WRITING

GARLAND NOTES

A collection of notes by Jenna Benton and Colonel Iverson Shavers may be found in their personal files, see references. Also, references letter to Curtis Tunnell, Executive Director of Texas Historical Commission and Rosco Shavers.

APPENDICES 1

Victoria Scott Patterson
Grandmother of Laura Shavers and her descendants
Siblings and descendants
recorded by
Laura G. Shavers in her own writing

Grand Mother of Laura
Victoria Paterson Born about
1830 died 1899 age 69. There were
there were 11 children born to
her: ~~Octavia~~ In New Boston

Jenna Knight Garland
Octavia Sparks Garland.
John Hunter
James Hunter
Charlie Shavers
Mattie Scott Keith.
William Scott
Clinton Scott
Sallie Scott
Edward Scott
Earnest Scott

Jenna Knight Garland mother
of eight children all of DeKalb
Names Effie Garland - Shavers
Born in New Boston Jossie Garland - Shavers
Born in DeKalb James Garland
" Hartwell Garland
" Smithie Garland - Hubbard
" Laura Garland Shavers
(Two passed as babies)
Jossie left one girl Ethel Shavers Be
Effie family names Harry, William

Millie — 6 children named: DeLaurel, Sherril Collins, Iverson James Collins, Tanyt— Sr, Dommie Collins, Terkie — Collins

Mattie — 3 children, Named; Chas Jr, Phillip — — —

Lenny Phillips
Mildred 5 children named: Gregory, Laura Gail, Raymond, Emerson, Kingston.

Jennie D. Shavers Benton 1 one Chil. name; Robert Calvin, Benton

Myrtle; 3 children; 1 Baumas the, Nydne ~~Collins~~, Myra, Laurel, Downs.

They were two children born To Ethel Shavers-Bell, Named Elois Bell, Iverson Bell.
Elois has five Children
Iverson has five, Dont Know names

Millie Shavers Collins
Mattie Shavers Johnson
Jemima V Shavers Burton
Lorenzo Shavers :- Six children
names — Hazel Shavers —
Stanley Shavers, Theodore
Shavers, Lorenzo Jr Shavers
Don Gloria Shavers, Leon
Shavers
Fred Shavers; Seven chil
Barbara Ann Shavers - Holla
Fred Shavers Jr, James Sha
Robert Lewis Shavers, Mari
Shavers, Kenneth Shav
Paul E. Shavers.
Helen Jackson :- Three Child
Robert Jackson, Walter Jack
Wylma Jackson. 2 children
Robert four children Walt
four children, Wylma
children. Laura Pearl - None
James Shavers :- one chi
Pamela Shavers
Iverson two children, name
Michael Shavers -

The following information was taken from a piece of paper found in an old shed. It was probably researched and prepared by Laura Pearl Shavers Sands.

Names	**Age**	**Wed**	**Spouse**	**Age**
Jim Polk-Garland	1850-1923	1872	Jennie Knight	1858-1888
I. Jossie Garland	1874-1893		I. William Shavers, Sr.	1868-1965
A. Ethel Shavers	18__-1918		A. Clayton Bell	18__-1970
1. Eloise Bell	1914		1. C. Barrett	
2. Iverson Bell	1917		2. Ethel Davis	
II. Mollie Garland	Baby			
III. Effie Garland	1876-19__		III. William Shavers, Sr.	1867-1965
IV. Jim Garland	1878-1957		IV. Zilphia Thornes	1886-19
V. Hart Garland	1880-1913		V. Lititia Estes	
A. Zether Garland	1802-19		A. Cornelius Webb	
1. Loys Webb	- 19		1.Nancy	
a. Alaistair Webb				
VI. Smithie Garland	1882-19		VI. John Hubbard, St.	18__-1936
VII. Charlie Garland	Baby			
VIII. Laura Garland	1886-1983		VIII. Robert Shavers	18__-1959
2nd Wife – no children				
Jim Polk Garland	Same	1896	Millie Walker	18__-19__

	Age	Wed	Spouse	Age
Jim Polk Garland	1850-1923	1872	Jennie Knight	1858-1888
I. Jossie Garland	1874-1893		I. William Shavers, Sr.	1867-1965
A. Ethel Shavers	18 -1918		A. Clayton Bell	18 -1970
1. Eloise Bell	1914		1.C. Barrett	
2. Iverson Bell	1917		2. Ethel Davis	
II. Mollie Garland	Baby			
III. Effie Garland	1876-19		III. William Shavers, Sr.	1867-1965
IV. Jim Garland	1878-1957		IV. Zilphia Thornes	1886-19
V. Hart Garland	1880-1913		V. Lititia Estes	
A. Zether Garland	1802-19		A. Cornelius Webb	
1. Loys Webb	-19		1. Nancy	
a. Alaistair Webb				
VI. Smithie Garland	1882-19		VI. John Hubbard, Sr.	18 -1936
VII. Charlie Garland	Baby			
VIII. Laura Garland	1886-1983		VII. Robert Shavers	18 -1959
2nd. Wife - no children				
Jim Polk Garland	Same	1896	Millie Walker	18 -19

v2n5 March 1917

THE GARLAND OAK

In the January issue of THE ALUMNUS we published the picture of a giant oak over the simple title, "Garland Oak on West Campus," and made no further remarks thereupon. Since then many parties have called our attention to the fact that the oak in question is no longer in existence, and the picture therefore does not represent the campus as it is. Our antiquary has made for us now an exhaustive investigation into the entire history of the Garland oak, and we give here some of his findings in a much abbreviated form.

It is true that the oak no longer stands. It was put out of existence in 1911 by Cap Alley and his cohorts, and the remains piled up in state along with the bones of many another outworn hero just back of Kissam Hall. The picture itself shows that the Garland oak had developed a very alarming tilt towards the west; it does not show what was also a fact, that a decay of many years standing had almost eaten out the base of it; and the two considerations were sufficient to convince any reasonable observer that the ancient tree was likely to go over in the course of any strong wind and was a menace to innocent passersby.

History centered about the Garland oak to a degree not equalled in the case of any other tree on the campus. (Incidentally the subject of campus trees might well inspire a volume from some loving Vanderbilt naturalist, for we doubt if there is another campus collection to equal it in all this country.) The name itself was applied to the tree from the fact that it stood just north of Chancellor Garland's house, now the home of Dr. Stevenson and the first of the residences on the road from West End through to the tennis courts after passing Kissam Hall. The old Chancellor set particular store by the oak which guarded the approach to his home. He placed boxes in it for the benefit of the squirrels, and he would not allow the birds which sang in it to be disturbed.

The Garland oak stood at the top of the hill on which the whole campus takes its commanding situation, and its position was indeed so conspicuous that various surveys were made from it as a starting point for the land round about. Forty years ago a road led westwards from Broad Street right through the campus towards the Garland oak. The road is still there, in a considerably improved state, but the oak which was once such a landmark no longer stands.

The oak figured prominently in deeds of conveyance, after the primitive fashion of locating real estate so much favored in Tennessee and Kentucky history. Most famous is a deed that is still preserved among the archives of the University, though the paper is yellow with age and brittle from the fire of 1905 through which it passed. The deed on the outside bears this inscription:

H. N. McTyeire, Trustee
To Deed
"The Vanderbilt University"
65 1-2 Acres—the
University Site
28 July, 1873.

The paper itself goes on to define "certain real estate," which had been made over to said H. N. McTyeire as Trustee for Central University and is herein conveyed to Vanderbilt University which has now succeeded said Central University; and the boundary lines are given with reference to a certain "overcup oak," which we can easily reckon from the description to have been identical with the tree that was to be known finally as the Garland oak.

Sic transit gloria mundi, our antiquary concludes.

BROADWAY ENTRANCE, WEST CAMPUS

VANDERBILT UNIVERSITY

Division of Public Affairs

May 7, 2010

Ms. Mattie Shavers Johnson
3511 Geneva Circle
Nashville, TN 37209

Dear Ms. Johnson:

Enclosed you will find information on the family of Landon Cabell Garland, Vanderbilt University's first chancellor. This material came from a biographical sketch written by one of Chancellor Garland's granddaughters. This, along with several other documents by and about Landon Garland, can be found and studied in Special Collections/University Archives located on the 21st Avenue side of the Jean and Alexander Heard Library located on Vanderbilt's campus.

Metered parking is available in the lot located between the library and Owen School of Management. The lot is directly across 21st Avenue from Panera Bread, San Antonio Taco Co., and Ben & Jerry's Ice Cream. There is also longer term parking directly across 21st Avenue from the library in Wesley Place Garage which can be entered from Scarritt Place.

I would be delighted to meet you at the library to show you all the Garland materials. In addition, we have in Kirkland Hall an oil portrait of Chancellor Garland painted by one of his granddaughters. Located in the Stevenson Science Library is a marble bust made by Enid Yandell. Chancellor Garland's gravesite is also located on the campus.

I am enclosing a copy of a photograph of Landon C. Garland. When I requested a scan of the photograph, I was reminded of the University Archives' policy regarding the publishing of photographs from the collection. In compliance with that policy, please check with Henry Shipman, Digital Imaging Specialist in Special Collections/University Archives at 322-2807. He will be happy to direct you through the process.

Best wishes to you on your book. And please give me a call if I can be of further help or meet you at the library.

Best regards,

Lyle Lankford

Lyle Lankford
Sr. Officer, University History & Protocol
Public Affairs
343-1579

405 Kirkland Hall
Nashville, Tennessee 37240

tel 615.343.1790
fax 615.322.4642
www.vanderbilt.edu/publicaffairs

An equal opportunity, affirmative action employer

Appendix

Madison County, Tennessee General Index to Deeds
March 23, 1821 – December 31, 1899

Page No. 18

Schedule 1.—Inhabitants in Precinct No 4, in the County of Bowie, State of Texas, enumerated by me on the 5 day of July, 1870.

Post Office: DeKalb

Wm L. Mabry, Ass't Marshal.

Inquiries numbered 7, 16, and 17 are not to be asked in respect to infants. Inquiries numbered 11, 12, 15, 16, 17, 19, and 20 are to be answered (if at all) merely by an affirmative mark, as /.

	Line	Dwelling No.	Family No.	Name	Age	Sex	Color	Occupation	Value of Real Estate	Value of Personal Estate	Place of Birth
	1			Henderson John	8	M	B				Tex
	2			Copper Robert	10	M	B				Tex
	3	126	128	Ingram M. L.	32	M	W	Farm Laborer	100	1000	Miss
	4			— Anna J	20	F	W	Keeping house			Tex
	5			— Francis E.	2	F	W				Tex
	6			— Lawrence S	2/12	M	W				Tex
	7			Collins William M	12	M	W	Farm Laborer			N.C.
	8	127	129	Haynes Polk	23	M	B	" "			Tenn
X	9			— Eliza	22	F	B	" "			Tenn
	10			— Margaret	4	F	B				Tex
	11			— Charley	1	M	B				Tex
X	12			— Mary	2/12	F	B				Tex
	13	128	130	Garland Alfred	20	M	B	Farm Laborer			Tenn
	14			— Sylla	18	F	B	" "			Tenn
	15	129	131	Garland James	70	M	B	" "			Va
X	16			— Ruth	52	F	M	Keeping house			Tenn
	17			— James P	21	M	B	Farm Laborer			Tenn
X	18			— Robert	17	M	B	" "			Tenn
	19			— Leander	15	M	B	" "			Tenn
	20			— Jane	18	F	B	" "			Tenn
X	21			— Tennessee	12	F	B	" "			Tenn
	22		132	Waller Prince	23	M	B	" "			S.C.
X	23			— Emily	17	F	B	" "			Tenn
X	24			— Sarah E	1	F	B				Tex
	25	130	133	Elwick James	27	M	B	Farm Laborer		200	Tenn
	26			— Frances	26	F	B	" "			Tenn
	27			— Robert	2	M	B				Tex
	28			Hogg Greene	16	M	B	Farm Laborer			Ala
	29	131	134	Garland Thomas	27	M	B	" "		125	Tenn
	30			— Sarah	29	F	B	" "			Tenn
	31			— Luke E.	8	M	B				Tex
	32			— Mary	3	F	B				Tex
	33			— Not named	1	M	B				Tex
	34	132	135	Brigham Wiley	27	M	B	Farm Laborer		125	Tex
	35			— Nancy	24	F	M	" "			Tenn
	36	133	136	Garland Benjamin	36	M	B	" "		100	Ala
	37			— Permelia	34	F	B	" "			Tenn
	38			— Lewis	9	M	B				Tex
	39			— Mary	7	F	B				Tex
	40			— Joseph	5	M	B				Tex

No. of dwellings, 8   No. of white females, 2   No. of males, foreign born, —
" " families, 7   " " colored males, 20   " " females, —
" " white males, 3   " " " females, 15   " " blind, —

7 of the children listed with astericks (x) are Ruth & Jim Garland's Children

ARCHIVES

Letter to Laura Garland Shavers from cousin Mattie Stone

Detroit 6 Mich
Aug 6-1961

My Dearest cousin; I guess it is about time I am ans your letter. Well through the mercy of God I am thankful to be here waiting for you to come If you don't get there in 1961 I hope be Gods will will see you in 1962 I am still able to read my Bible and pray although I know I don't pray as often as I should. David prayed three times a day. David said Thy word is a lamp unto my feet and a light unto my path way. David was a man after Gods own heart, as you know we get our spiritual food through the study of the Bible and pray. Oh yes I must tell you I had to friends from Camden Ark. my old home town the late Dr. J.A. Clarks widdow Alberta Clark Miss Bessie

2

moore also from Camden her
mother and I are very Close friends
we were neighbors over 30 yrs.
they Came July 10th stayed two wk
Mrs Clark has a sister and Bro
that live here Miss Bessie moore
has relatives living here Mildred
saw Myrtle ~~some~~ a few days
ago they ran upon each other
accidently my younger son
is still laid off from work
has been since Nov. 1960 he
draws Compasation I hope I will
live to send you as much as $5.00
~~to pay~~ to help with fenceing with
the Cemetery what little extra
Change that is given me it
seemes I have to use it for thing
I have to have for my self. I
write quite a bit stamps stationery
I use a lot of chewing gum I use
one of those large tubes of white
vaseline 49¢ tube to oil my body
orders from the Dr. keep my skin

3

from getting dry one last two
wks a tube of toilet Landlin
squib for my foot between my
toes and heel to keep them from
getting sore a small tube cost
39¢ I use one a wk. Mildred
is the only one of my three
children here that works
regular my older daughter live in
Cleveland the other children has
to help her always have she
has so many children and grand
children Oh yes Mrs Clark is a
very close friend of Ethel Mc
Peters Mrs Clark told me Lillian
Fields ~~we~~ husband passed some
time ago I hope [illegible]
[illegible]
Essie Showers and Sister Effie [illegible]
also Jimmie C. Ma was sick on
Jimmie C. almost [illegible] years but
Jimmie C stuck to her mother
she had no help where is Lee Dotson
is he living how is Zilpha give my

4

love to her is Madie Pirkey still
living? I heard Vashtie pass in
1956 & I heard Clara Jones passed
Nora sister Nettie passed all these
Aunt Jane Waller's girls Laura
girl you are blessed and think
Cousin Effie tell her she may
live to be [illegible] you to grandpa
Jim my mother and your daddy's
father grandma said one day sh
[illegible] missed him he had striped off
all his clothes sitting besible a
big tree when she found him said
Lord Jim what are you doing
out her. he said and I quote I am
out here to see and be seen just
like he came into the world. did
you know he was a full blood
African his mother and father
was brought from Africa on
a boat as slaves could not
speak one word of english
my grandpa daddy Jim as they
called him was born to them

6—

after they were brought to america
Well I know you would like to
know how is it mattie know so
much. Well grand Ruth Garland
lived with my mother most of
the time I would hear them
talk you know how kids evesdrop.
older people sometime I would
hear Uncle Robt. and mamma
talk did you know my mother
was the first negro school
teacher that taught in that
little log cabin grand Ruth stole
her education nursing master Jacs
children he had by his white
wife her half Bro and sisters old
man Joe Garland miss mary and
Margeret they liked her because
she was good to them grandma
Ruth taught Mama and uncle Robt
because they were anxious to lear.
they could read and spell every thin
in the blue back spelling book they
were educated my mother went to scho
4 mo. in her life at that time they had a

6

white teacher why I am writing this to you myrtle told me one of her brothers wanted the history of the garlands why I know my mother uncle Robt G and Ruth R would sit talk so much about those days some things they tell us things they wanted us to know without your concent I will not tell them any thing I did tell myrtle I can't remember your mother how she looked she was as white as any white woman strait sandy hair hung almost to her waist line I can only remember two thing one sunday she and mama had been to church mamma went in the kitchen to cook dinner after gett-ing back from church she went to cook some biscuits she had no soda she sent Clem Jessie I follow them after some soda aunt Jennie had undressed was bare feet her hair

7

was loose hanging down her
back she was under a peach
tree with a pan in her hand
gathering peaches a big old ind
ian peach red and juicy and
I do remember when she was on
her death bed leaning on her
elbow eating a piece of dried
smoked beef she called me to the
bed and ~~to~~ pinched off a piece
and gave me I remember Dr
Ball Came aunt Mary anthnie
caried me out of the room
we sat on a bench beside the
house aunt Mary anthnie
had a ~~ris~~ boil under her
arm Dr. Ball Lanced it I can't
remember anything else only
aunt Jennie would say King
fine for rener and groan I
heard them say what caused her
death miscarraige I hope you don't
think I am crazy I will close
here from your devoted Cousin
Mattie Stone

when I started this letter
I did not intend to write
all this I wish Effie
could come with you

Mittie Stone
3288 Cortland
Detroit 6 Mich.

APPENDICES II

Notes that came from Hazel Atkinson when visiting the author

JENNA KNIGHT AND SARAH

SARH KNIGHT + FRANK

PINKY Ware

MARRIED

FRANCIS — HARGETTE C. ELLIS SR.

ACIE, ~~RICHARD~~, ALONZO SR, ZONA BELL, EVA BELL

HAZEL

HHELAN

MCKINLEY

RICHARD — JAQUALINE, RICHARD II "SAMSON"

ALONZO SR — ABRAM, ALONZO III

MABLE FRANCINE — SOLOMON, JERICHA, JARIUS, KEZIAH

WILLIAM HARGET — WILLIAM SR, MCKINLEY BARRET, DAVID, BLAINE

JUANITA HELEN

ESTHER

PEARL

ZONA

HAZEL

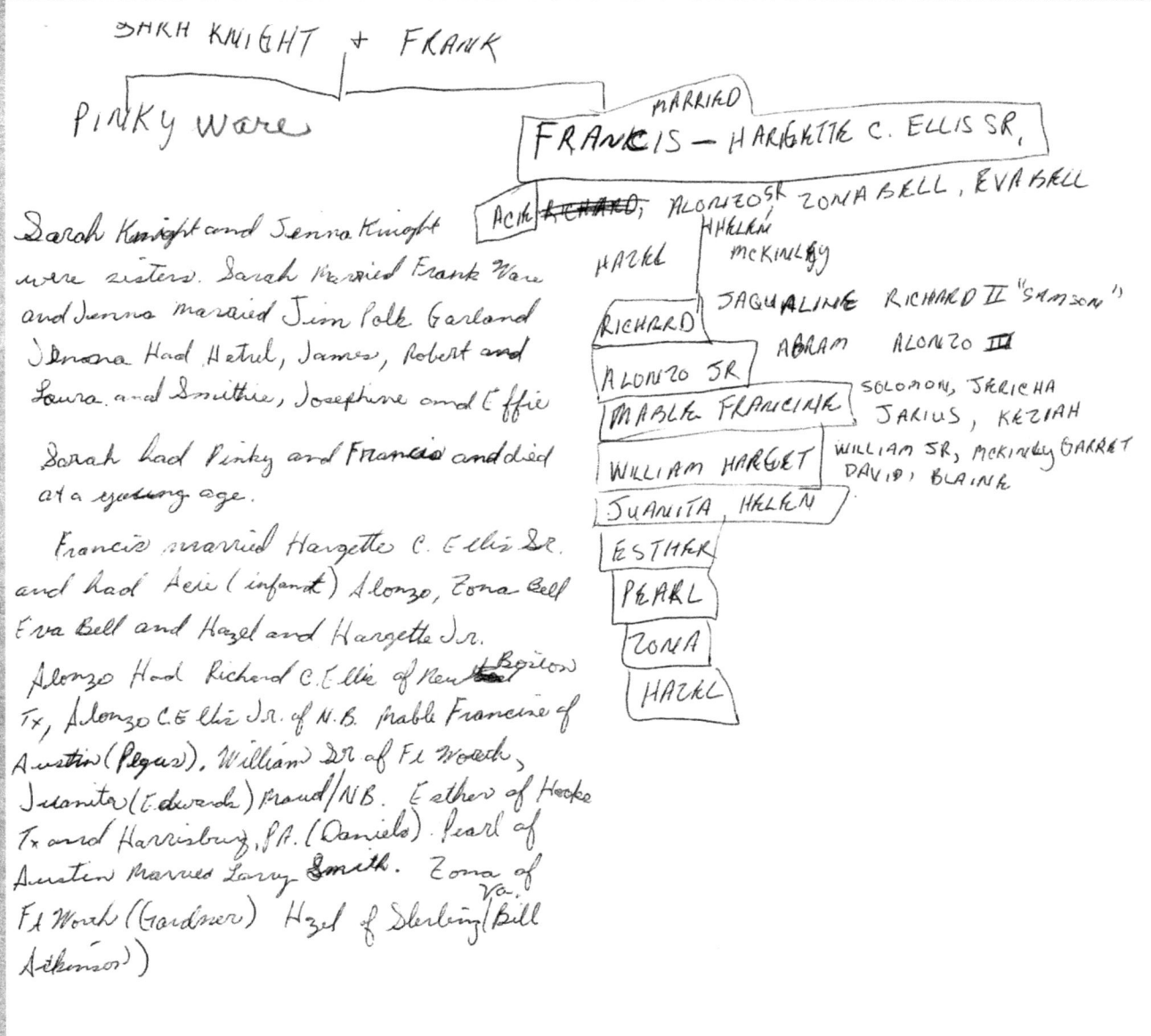

Sarah Knight and Jenna Knight were sisters. Sarah Married Frank Ware and Jenna married Jim Polk Garland. Jenna Had Hetul, James, Robert and Laura and Smithie, Josephine and Effie

Sarah had Pinky and Francis and died at a young age.

Francis married Hargette C. Ellis Sr. and had Acie (infant) Alonzo, Zona Bell Eva Bell and Hazel and Hargette Jr. Alonzo Had Richard C. Ellis of New Boston Tx, Alonzo C.Ellis Jr. of N.B. Mable Francine of Austin (Pegues). William Sr of Ft Worth, Juanita (Edwards) Maud/NB. Esther of Hooks Tx and Harrisburg, PA. (Daniels). Pearl of Austin Married Larry Smith. Zona of Ft Worth (Gardner) Hazel of Sterling Va. (Bill Atkinson))

Hazel Elbin atchison
From Virginia —

HAZEL E. ATKINSON
135 ENVIRONS RD
STERLING, VA 20165
703-406-0471 (H)

703-517-9604 (C)

JENNA

SARAH KNIGHT – FRANK

LAURA | EFFIE | SMITHIE

ROBERT SHAVERS

JOSEPHINE | ROBERT | JAMES

JAMES + JEMIMA'S KNIGHT CHILDREN "[redacted]"
POLK GARLAND

SHAVERS

1 LORENZO — 6 STANLEY, HAZEL, JIMMIE, LORENZO JR., "TEDDY" THEODORE, DON GLORIA

2 FRED — BARBARA ANNE, "F.G." FRED GARLAND

JAMES — PAMELA

3 HELEN — ROBERT, WILLMA JEAN, WALTER

LAURA PEARL — NO CHILDREN

MILLIE + — DELAURA, SHERRY, JAMES, TANYA, TIERI

3 *MATTIE — CHARLES WILLIAM, PHILLIP, LEVETTE

3 MYRTLE *

5 * MILDRED — RENARD, ROY, GREGORY, EMERSON "DAUGHTER"

IVERSON — MICHAEL FRANCIS

JENNA VI — ROBERT, BRIAN

Jennie Knight, wife of
James (Jim Polk). Garland
and
Sarah Knight, wife of
Frank Ware

Sarah Knight and Jennie Knight
were sisters. — Sarah married
Frank Ware and Jennie married
James (Jim Polk Garland
Jennie had Hartwell, James
Robert, Smithie, Josephine, Effie
Laura
Sarah had, Pinky and Francis
She died at a young age.
Francis married Hargitt Ellis Sr.
and had Arie (an infant), Alonzo
Zona Bell and Eva Bell and
Hazel and Hargitt Jr.
Alonzo had Richard C. Ellis of
New Boston, Alonzo Ellis, Jr of
New Boston, Mable Francine (over)

of Austin, William Jr. of Ft Worth
Juanita Edwards of — of New
Boston
Esther of Lockhart, Texas and
Harrisburg, Pa. — (Daniels)
Pearl of Austin, Tx.
Pres (-?) Leroy Smith
Iona of Ft Worth (Gardner)
Hazel of Sterling (Bill)
Ackmon (?)
See appendix no —

APPENCICES III

Madison County, Tennessee

General Index to Deeds

March 23, 1821 - December 31, 1899

MADISON COUNTY, TENNESSEE

General Index to Deeds—INDIRECT—March 23, 1821 to Dec. 31, 1899

GRANTEE	GRANTOR	KIND OF INSTRUMENT	RECORDED BOOK	RECORDED PAGE	DATE OF INSTRUMENT	DATE FILED	DESCRIPT
Garland, John, C	Kirby, Jas. M	Deed	9	564	12/6/1844	3/12/1845	80A, R 2, Sec.
Garland, John, C. et.al.	Angus, Alexander,	Release	11	159	12/7/1846	12/21/1846	Real Propert
Garland, John, C	Simmons, James, et.al.	Trans.	12	254	4/17/1847	1/11/1849	Real Propert
Garland, John, C	Alexander, Mary, et.al.	Trans.	12	254	4/17/1847	1/11/1849	Real Propert
Garland, J.C	Murchison, John	W.D	16	41	9/4/1851	9/11/1852	491 A, D 1
Garland, John	Jelks, John, R.	Shff.D	17	745	8/27/1849	2/12/1855	91 A
Garland, John, C	Johnson, Joseph	W.D	18	17	5/18/1848	3/5/1855	195 A, D 9
Garland, John, C. et.ux. Nancy	Fry, Katy, et.al.	Div. D	21	364	10/30/1858	5/28/1859	100 A, No.9
Garland, John, C.M	Rowlett, John, J	W.D	17	393	10/[illegible]7/1853	9/5/1854	200 A, D 17
Garland, John, C.M	Robertson, John, C	W.D	17	586	12/1/1854	12/9/1854	140 A, D 1-1
Garland, John, C. M	Connelly, George, A. et.al.	Exr. D	18	144	5/24/1855	6/6/1855	32 A, D 17
Garland, John, C.M	Connally, George, A. et.al.	Exr. D	18	141	5/24/1855	6/6/1855	299 A, D 17
Garland, John, C.M	Connally, George, A. et.al.	Exr. D	18	143	5/24/1855	6/6/1855	77 A, D 17
[illegible]d, John, C.M	Connelly, Robert, A. et.al.	Exr. D	18	144	5/24/1855	6/6/1855	32 A, D 17
Garland, John, C.M	Connally, Robt. A. et.al.	Exr. D	18	141	5/24/1855	6/6/1855	299 A, D 17
Garland, John, C.M.	Connally, Robert, A. et.al.	Exr. D	18	143	5/24/1855	6/6/1855	77 A, D 17
Garland, John, C.M	Lancaster, Samuel	W.D	19	97	6/14/1856	9/22/1856	Market St.
Garland, J.C.M	Croom, Elizabeth,	Release	19	506	3/3/1857	4/4/1857	Dower Real
Garland, John, C.M	Gaines, R.L.	W.D	19	364	1/19/1857	2/7/1857	Market St.
Garland, J.C.M	Greer, T. M	W.D	21	647	9/12/1859	2/4/1860	3 Tracts
Garland, J.C.M	Rogers, A.S	W.D	23	169	1/15/1862	1/20/1862	Lafayette-
Garland, John, C.M. et.al.	Harris, George, N	W.D	24	183	2/28/1866	7/3/1866	
Garland, J.C.M	Thees, F.D	W.D	26	25	4/[illegible]7/1868	4/30/1868	Main-Mark
Garland, John, C.M. et.al.	Reavis, James, M. et.al.	Part.D	27	211	9/16/1869	9/18/1869	Lafayette
Garland, J.C.M	Anderson, Robert, H.	Deed	28	14	5/26/1870	5/26/1870	House and
Garland, John, C.M	Boyce, Wm.H	W.D	28	115	8/12/1870	8/12/1870	273 A
Garland, John, C.M	Ackerman, E. et.al.	Decree	28	338	3/17/1870	12/9/1870	Lot
Garland, John, C.M ½	Chancery Court, et.al.	Decree	28	338	3/17/1870	12/9/1870	Lot
Garland, John, C.M	Deberry, Allen, et.al.	"	28	338	3/17/1870	12/9/1870	"
[illegible]and, John, C. M	Rosenthal, Henrietta, et.al.	"	28	338	3/17/1870	12/9/1870	"
Garland, John, C..M.	Rosenthal, Julius, et.al.	Decree	28	338	3/17/1870	12/9/1870	Lot
Garland, John, C.M	Gentry, J.B	W.D	28	556	3/6/1871	3/15/1871	Lot, Coll
Garland, J. C.M	Fallen, Thomas	W.D	30	317	5/29/1872	9/27/1872	Tract, Mil
Garland, J.C.M	Hubbard, Samuel, R. et.al.	W.D	30	560	1/15/1873	1/30/1873	Main St.
Garland, J.C.M	Hubbard, Benjamin, H. et.al.	W.D	30	560	1/15/1873	1/30/1873	"
Garland, J.C.M	Lane, Alice et.vir. John, J. et.al	W.D	30	561	1/20/1873	1/31/1873	Main St.
Garland, J.C. M	Salter, Nannie B. et.vir. T.C	W.D	30	561	1/20/1873	1/31/1873	Main St.
Garland, J.C.M	Hubbard, Ali ce, et.al.	W.D	30	561	1/20/1873	1/31/1873	"
Garland, J.C.M.	Hubbard, Nannie B. et.al.	W.D	30	561	1/20/1873	1/31/1873	Main St.
Garland, John, C.M	Hubbard Lula, P. et.al.	W.D	30	598	2/5/1873	2/13/1873	Main St.
Garland, J.C.M	Hubbard, Samuel, R. et.al.	W.D	30	598	2/5/1873	2/13/1873	Main St.
Garland, J. C.M	Lane, J.J. et.ux. Allie, et.al.	W.D	30	598	2/5/1873	2/13/1873	"
Garland, J.C.M	Wise, Frank, P. et.ux. Mary, et.al.	W.D	30	598	2/5/1873	2/13/1873	"
Garland, J.C.M	Allis, Lula, et.vir. Geo.B	W.D	30	598	2/5/1873	2/13/1873	"
Garland, John, C.M.	Salter, Thos.C. et.ux. Nannie C	W.D	30	598	2/5/1873	2/13/1873	"

GRANTEE	GRANTOR	KIND OF INSTRUMENT	RECORDED BOOK	RECORDED PAGE	DATE OF INSTRUMENT	DATE FILED
Gardner, Wm. F	Gardner, Joseph, H.et.al.	Decree	29	613	1/4/1871	3/20/1872
Gardner, Wm. F	County Court, et.al.	"	29	613	1/4/1871	3/20/1872
Gardner, Wm. F	Haltom, Nathan, et.al.	Decree	29	613	1/4/1871	3/20/1872
Gardner, Wm. F	Haltom, Mary J.et.al.	Decree	29	613	1/4/1871	3/20/1872
Gardner, Wm. F	Haltom, Joseph, N.et.al.	"	29	613	1/4/1871	3/20/1872
Gardner, Wm. F	Haltom, Martha, E.et.al.	Decree	29	613	1/4/1871	3/20/1872
Gardner, Wm. F	Haltom, John.S.et.al.	Release	32	518	8/11/1873	10/5/1874
Gardner, Wm. F	Haltom, John, S	Release	32	519	8/11/1873	10/5/1874
Gardner, W.F	Haltom, Sarah, EW	W.D	28	266	8/23/1866	11/11/1870
Gardner, W. F	Gardner, Jas. H. et.al.	Decree	29	408	11/26/1871	1/6/1872
Gardner, W.F	Tharpe, Wm.A.et.al.	"	29	408	11/16/1871	1/6/1872
Gardner, W. F	Haltom, Wm. H.et.al.	"	29	408	11/16/1871	1/6/1872
Gardner, W.F	Haltom, Martha, E.et.al.	"	29	408	11/16/1871	1/6/1872
Gardner, W. F	Haltom, Joseph, N.et.al.	Decree	29	408	11/16/1871	1/6/1872
Gardner, W. F	Chancery Court, et.al.	"	29	408	11/16/1871	1/6/1872
Gardner, W. F	Haltom, Nathan, et.al.	Decree	29	408	11/16/1871	1/6/1872
Gardner, W.F	Haltom, Mary J. et.al.	"	29	408	11/16/1871	1/6/1872
Gardner, W F	Haltom, Nathan, et.al.	W. D	32	517	4/11/1872	10/5/1874
Gardner, W. F	Haltom, Nathan, .et.al.	Q.C.D	32	519	8/11/1873	10/5/1874
Gardner, W. F	Haltom, Nathan, et.al.	Deed	32	520	8/11/1873	10/5/1874
Gardner, W.F	Haltom, Elisha, S.et.al.	Admr. D	32	517	4/11/1872	10/5/1874
Gardner, W. F	Haltom, Berlinda, et.al.	Deed	32	520	8/11/1873	10/5/1874
Gardner, W.F	Haltom, John.S.et.al.	Admr.D	32	517	4/11/1872	10/5/1874
Gardner, W.F	Haltom, N.et.al.	Q.C.D	32	518	8/11/1873	10/5/1874
Gardner, W.F	Haltom, JohnS.et.ux.Susan, A	Deed	36	399	8/15/1877	3/3/1879
Gardner, W.F	Haltom, J. N.et.al.	W.D	45	519	10/29/1888	10/29/1888
Gardner, W.F	Rice, W.A.et.ux.M.E.et.al.	W.D	45	519	10/29/1888	10/29/1888
Gardner, W. F	Fogg, A.B.et.ux.M.J.et.al.	W.D	45	519	10/29/1888	10/29/1888
Garland, Berry, P	Teague, J.R.et.ux Susan.A	W.D	58	59	6/21/1895	6/28/1899
Garland, C.M.et.al.	Connally, G.A.et.al.	Decree	17	186	7/16/1851	2/23/1854
Garland, E.W	Garland, Martha, et.al.	W.D	25	215	1/8/1867	1/8/1867
Garland, E.W	Garland, Ann, et.al.	W.D	25	215	1/8/1867	1/8/1867
Garland, E. W	Garland, J.D.R.et.al.	W.D	27	130	4/17/1869	7/21/1869
Garland, E. W	Garland, John.C.et.al.	W.D	27	130	4/17/1869	7/21/1869
Garland, Edward, W	Hall, Claudius, B.et.al.	W.D	26	618	6/28/1854	3/31/1869
Garland, Edward, W	Hall, Selena, J.et.al.	W.D	26	618	6/28/1854	3/31/1869
Garland, Edward, W	Sanford, William. A.et.ux.Eliza B	W.D	26	619	8/5/1854	3/31/1869
Garland, Edward, W	Garland.Edward, et.al.	W.D	26	619	8/5/1854	3/31/1869
Garland, H.W.et.al.	Angus, Alexander	Trans.	11	159	12/7/1846	12/21/184
Garland, John C.et.al.	Hill, Jacob	W.D	3	485	3/6/1834	3/8/1834
Garland, J.et.al.	Herron, A.A	W.D	6	175	8/6/1835	8/6/1835
Garland, J.et.al.	Herron, A. H	W.D	6	176	8/6/1838	8/6/1838
Garland, John, C	Chalmers, John, G	W.D	6	316	12/24/1835	12/4/183
Garland, John, C, et.al.	Smith, John, D	W.D	7	458	9/25/1840	6/1/1841
Garland, John, C	Aldridge, Lemuel	W.D	9	171	7/25/1842	12/2/184

Page No. 18

Inquiries numbered 7, 16, and 17 are not to be asked in respect to infants. Inquiries numbered 11, 12, 15, 16, 17, 19, and 20 are to be answered (if at all) merely by an affirmative mark, as /.

SCHEDULE 1.—Inhabitants in Precinct No. 4, in the County of Bowie, State of Texas, enumerated by me on the 5 day of July 1870.

Post Office: De Kalb

Wm. L. Mabry, Ass't Marshal.

	Dwelling-houses numbered in the order of visitation (1)	Families numbered in the order of visitation (2)	The name of every person whose place of abode on the first day of June, 1870, was in this family (3)	Age (4)	Sex (5)	Color (6)	Profession, Occupation, or Trade of each person, male or female (7)	Value of Real Estate (8)	Value of Personal Estate (9)	Place of Birth (10)
1			Henderson John	8	M	B				Tex
2			Copper Robert	10	M	B				Tex
3	126	128	Ingram M. L.	32	M	W	Farm Laborer	100	1000	Miss
4			— Anna J	20	F	W	Keeping house			Tex
5			— Francis E.	2	F	W				Tex
6			— Lawrence S	7/12	M	W				Tex
7			Collins William M	12	M	W	Farm Laborer			N.C.
8	127	129	Haynes Polk	23	M	B	" "			Tenn
9			— Eliza	22	F	B	" "			Tenn
10			— Margaret	4	F	B				Tex
11			— Charley	1	M	B				Tex
12			— Mary	2/12	F	B				Tex
13	128	130	Garland Alfred	20	M	B	Farm Laborer			Tenn
14			— Sylla	18	F	B	" "			Tenn
15	129	131	Garland James	70	M	B	" "			Miss
16			— Ruth	52	F	M	Keeping house			Tenn
17			— James P	21	M	B	Farm Laborer			Tenn
18			— Robert	17	M	B	" "			Tenn
19			— Leander	15	M	B	" "			Tenn
20			— Jane	18	F	B	" "			Tenn
21			— Tennessee	12	F	B	"			Tenn
22		132	Waller Prince	23	M	B	" "			S.C.
23			— Emily	17	F	B	" "			Tenn
24			— Sarah S	1	F	B				Tex
25	130	133	Gwink James	27	M	B	Farm Laborer		200	Tenn
26			— Frances	26	F	B	" "			Tenn
27			— Robert	2	M	B				Tex
28			Hogg Greene	16	M	B	Farm Laborer			Ark
29	131	134	Garland Thomas	37	M	B	" "		125	Tenn
30			— Sarah	29	F	B	"			Tenn
31			— Lefie E.	8	M	B				Tex
32			— Mary	3	F	B				Tex
33			— Not named	1	M	B				Tex
34	132	135	Brigham Wiley	27	M	B	Farm Laborer		125	Tex
35			— Nancy	24	F	M	" "			Tenn
36	133	136	Garland Benjamin	36	M	B	" "		100	Ala
37			— Permelia	34	F	B	" "			Tenn
38			— Lewis	9	M	B				Tex
39			— Mary	7	F	B				Tex
40			— Joseph	5	M	B				Tex

No. of dwellings, 8 — No. of white females, 2 — No. of males, foreign born, ——
" " families, 9 — " " colored males, 20 — " " females, ——
" " white males, 3 — " " " females, 15 — " " blind, ——

No. of insane, ——

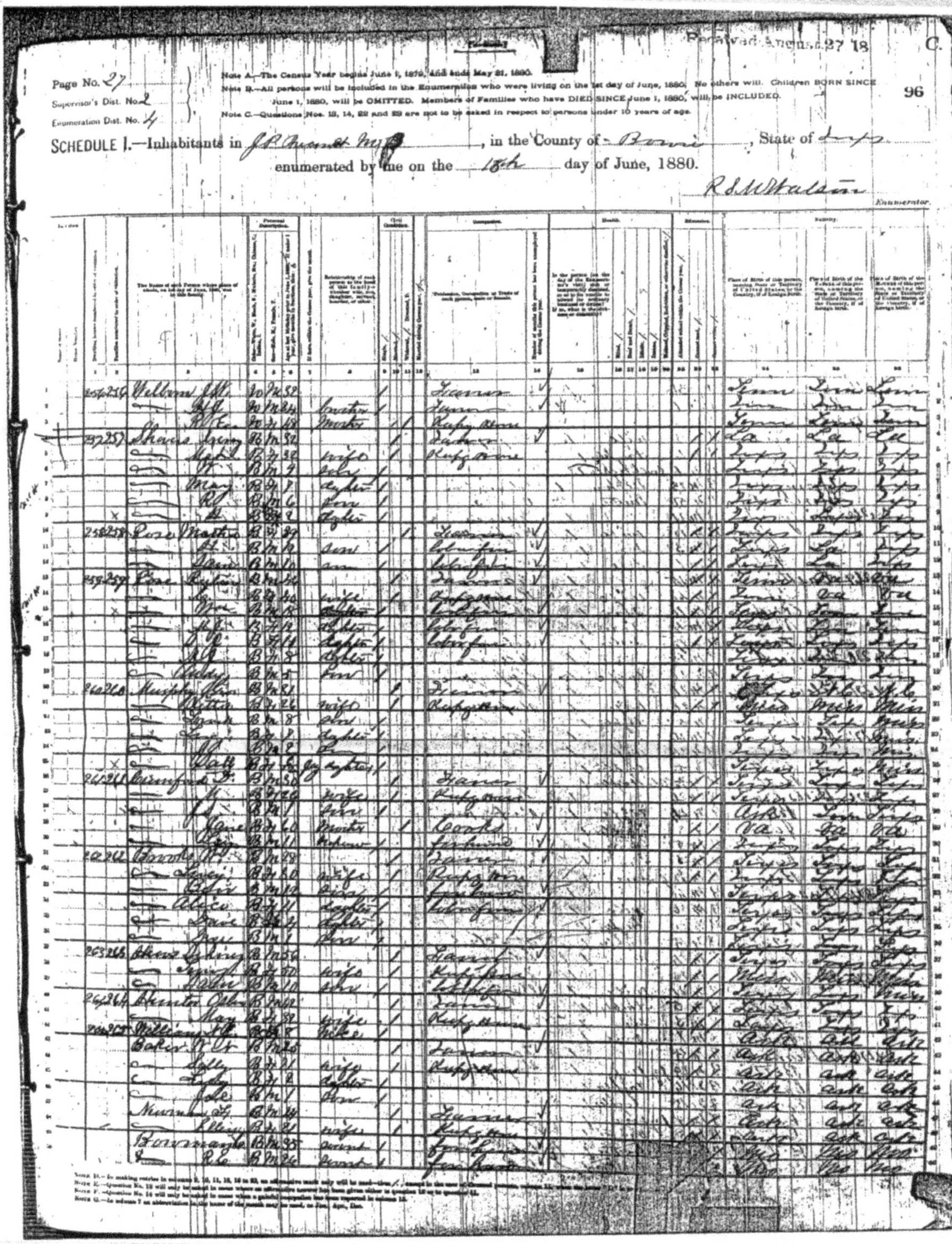

Received August 27 18 C.

Page No. 27
Supervisor's Dist. No. 2
Enumeration Dist. No. 4

Note A.—The Census Year begins June 1, 1879, and ends May 31, 1880.
Note B.—All persons will be included in the Enumeration who were living on the 1st day of June, 1880. No others will. Children BORN SINCE June 1, 1880, will be OMITTED. Members of Families who have DIED SINCE June 1, 1880, will be INCLUDED.
Note C.—Questions Nos. 13, 14, 22 and 23 are not to be asked in respect to persons under 10 years of age.

96

SCHEDULE 1.—Inhabitants in J.P. [illegible], in the County of Bowie, State of Texas, enumerated by me on the 18th day of June, 1880.

R. S. M. Watson, Enumerator.

1900 CENSUS

Microfilm Roll No. ______

State TEXAS

County BOWIE

Town/Township PCT. #3

Date ______

Supv. Dist. No. ______ Sheet No. 4

Enum. Dist. No. 9 Page No. ______

LOCATION				NAME		PERSONAL DESCRIPTION									NATIVITY			CITIZENSHIP			OCCUPATION		EDUCATION						
Street	House No.	Dwelling No.	Family No.	of each person whose place of abode on June 1, 1900, was in this family	Relation to head of family	Color	Sex	Month of birth	Year of birth	Age	Single, married, widowed, divorced	No. of years married	Mother of how many children	Number of these children living	Place of birth	Place of birth of father	Place of birth of mother	Year of immigration to U.S.	No. of years in U.S.	Naturalization	Occupation	No. of months not employed	Attended school (months)	Can read	Can write	Can speak English	Home owned or rented	Home owned free or mortgaged	Farm or house
		76	80	SHAVERS, IVERSON	HEAD	B	M	2	1852	48	M	30			LA	LA	LA				FARMER			YES	NO	YES	O	F	FA
				" , MATTIE	WIFE	B	F	3	1853	47	M	30	6	4	TX	ALA	VA							YES	YES	YES			
				" , ROBERT	SON	B	M	10	1876	23	S				TX	LA	TX				DAY LABORER			YES	YES	YES			
				STOKES, WILLIS	GND SON	B	M	11	1887	12	S				TX	AR ~~LA~~	TX				DAY LABORER		4	YES	YES	YES			
				STOKES, ETHEL	GND DAU	B	F	8	1893	6	S				TX	AR	TX							NO	NO	YES			

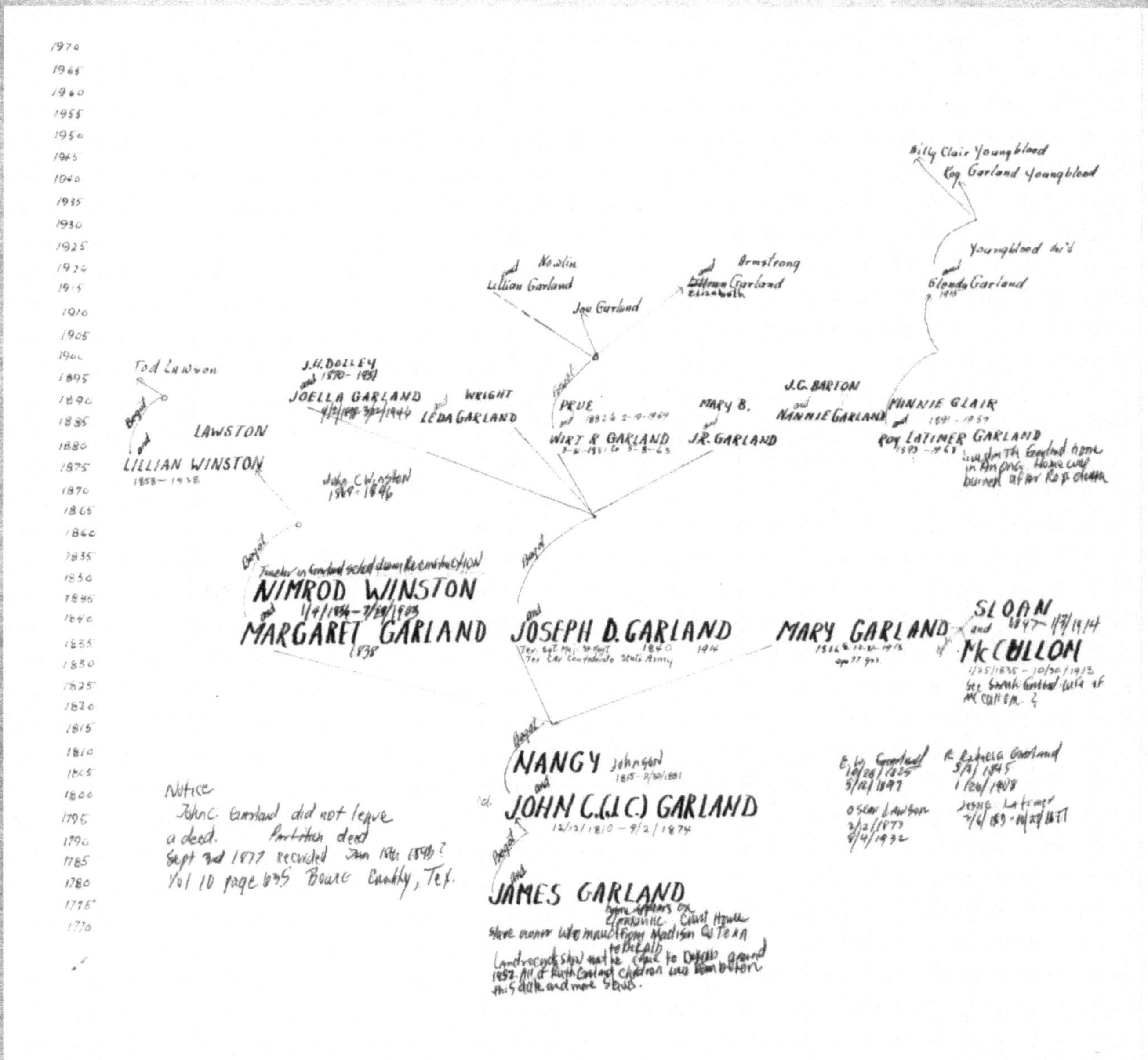
Billy Clair Youngblood
Roy Garland Youngblood
Youngblood
Glenda Garland
Nowlin
Lillian Garland
Armstrong
Elizabeth Garland
Joe Garland
Tod Lawson
J.H. DOLLEY
1870 - 1951
JOELLA GARLAND
WRIGHT
LEDA GARLAND
PRUE
WIRT R GARLAND
MARY B.
J.R. GARLAND
J.C. BARTON
NANNIE GARLAND
MINNIE CLAIR
1891 - 1959
ROY LATIMER GARLAND
LAWSTON
LILLIAN WINSTON
1858 - 1938
John C Winston
NIMROD WINSTON
1/4/1834 - 7/28/1903
MARGARET GARLAND
1838
JOSEPH D. GARLAND
1840
1914
Tex. Sgt. Maj.
Tex Cav Confederate State Army
MARY GARLAND
SLOAN
McCULLOM
1/25/1835 - 10/30/1913
NANCY Johnson
JOHN C. (J.C.) GARLAND
12/12/1810 - 9/2/1874
JAMES GARLAND
Notice
John C. Garland did not leave
a deed. Partition deed
Sept 3rd 1877 recorded
Vol 10 page 635 Bowie County, Tex.
Oscar Lawson
R. Rebecca Garland

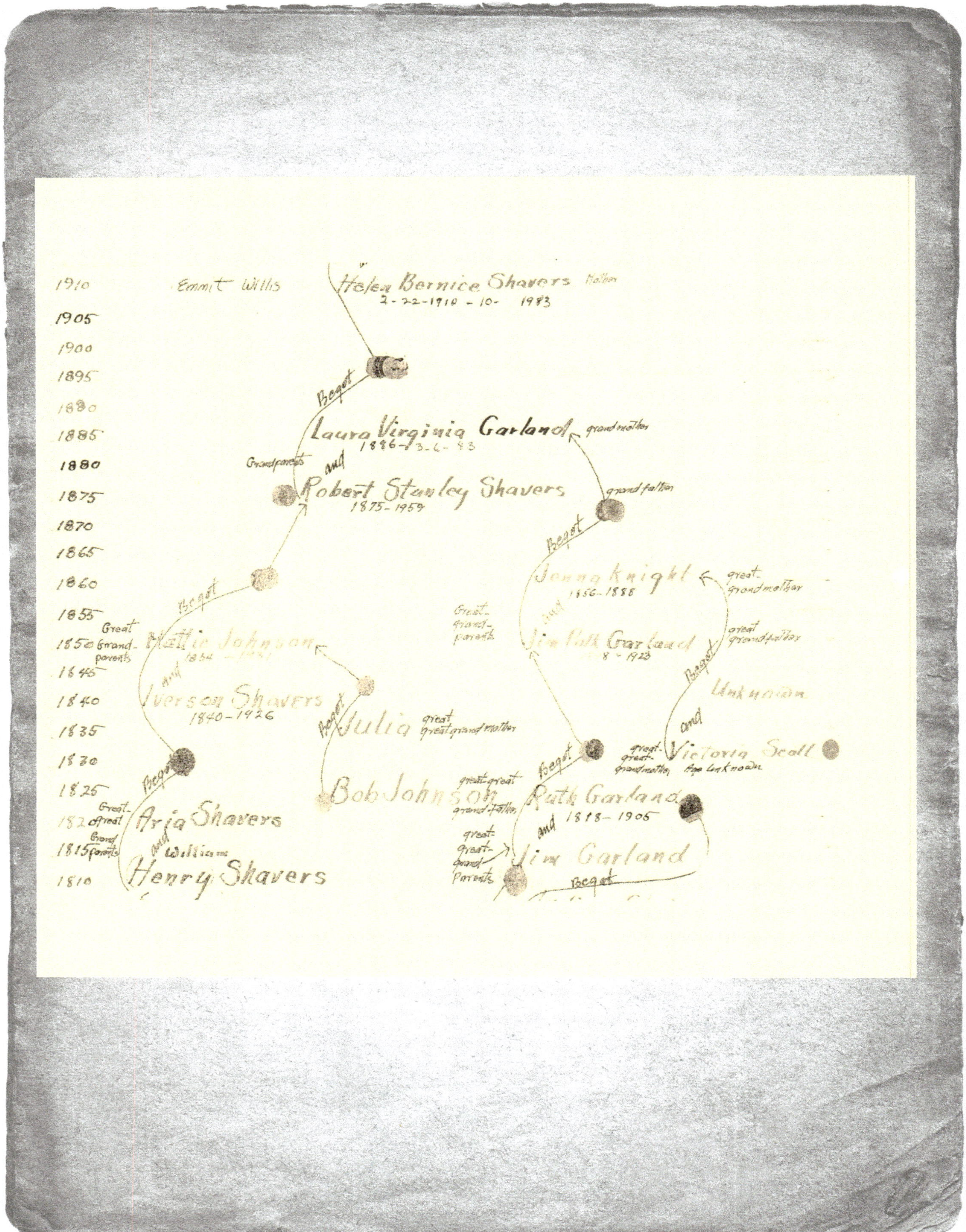
1910
1905
1900
1895
1885
1880
1875
1870
1865
1860
1855
1850
1840
1835
1830
1825
1815
1810
Emmit Willis
Helen Bernice Shavers
Mother
2-22-1910 - 10- 1983
Begot
Laura Virginia Garland
grandmother
Grandparents
and
Robert Stanley Shavers
1875-1959
grand father
Begot
Great Grand-parents
Iverson Shavers
1840-1926
Julia
great great grand mother
Bob Johnson
great-great grand-father
great grandmother
great grandfather
Begot
Unknown
and
Victoria Scott
great-great-grandmother
Begot
Ruth Garland
1818-1905
and
Jim Garland
Begot
great-great-grand Parents
Aria Shavers
and
William
Henry Shavers
Begot

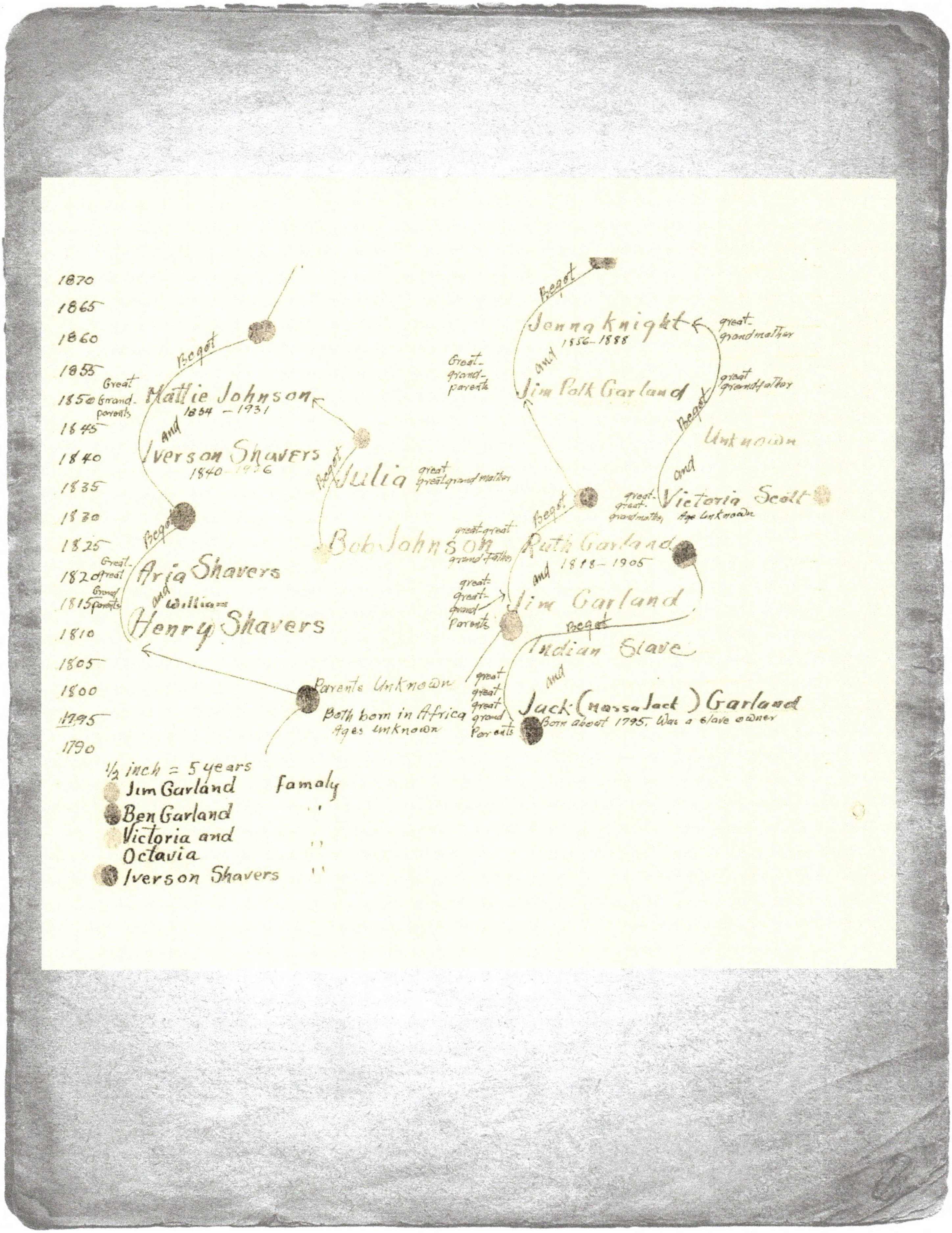
1870
1865
1860
1855
1850
1845
1840
1835
1830
1825
1820
1815
1810
1805
1800
1795
1790
Begot
Great Grand-parents
Mattie Johnson
1854 - 1931
and
Iverson Shavers
1840 - 1936
Begot
Julia
great great grand mother
Bob Johnson
great-great grand Father
Begot
Great-Great Grand parents
Aria Shavers
and
William
Henry Shavers
Parents Unknown
Both born in Africa
Ages unknown
Begot
Jenna Knight
1856 - 1888
great-grandmother
Great-grand-parents
and
Jim Polk Garland
great grandfather
Begot
Unknown
and
great-great-grandmother
Victoria Scott
Age Unknown
Begot
Ruth Garland
1818 - 1905
and
great-great-grand Parents
Jim Garland
Begot
Indian Slave
and
great great great grand Parents
Jack (Massa Jack) Garland
Born about 1795. Was a slave owner
1/2 inch = 5 years
Jim Garland famaly
Ben Garland
Victoria and Octavia
Iverson Shavers

Johnson retells history of medical school

Charles W. Johnson, Sr.

By LEW K. COHN
News Editor

Dr. Charles W. Johnson Sr. devoted more than 40 years of his life to the development and promotion of his beloved Meharry Medical College, the nation's largest private predominantly African-American medical school.

From creating the college's renown sickle cell research program to initiating the college's School of Graduate Studies, Johnson

Johnson's final work on earth was to write the definitive history of the Nashville, Tenn.-based school, entitled *The Spirit of a Place Called Meharry: The Strength of Its Past to Shape the Future.*

After Johnson passed away at age 77 on Aug. 18, 1999, his beloved wife, the former Mattie Shavers of the Garland Community near DeKalb, saw to it that the book was published. The book is now available from Hillsboro Press and Providence House Publishers of Franklin, Tenn.

"It took him about 10 years to complete the book after he retired," Mattie Johnson said. "A great deal of that time was spent doing all of the research and compiling all of the information he needed.

"He always felt a need to develop the school and felt that it was his responsibility to see to it. There were so many other things that he did and so many programs he helped institute to benefit the students. It has been said that he did more to develop and advance the medical school than anyone else on the campus."

What makes Meharry College remarkable is that nearly half of all black physicians and dentists currently practicing in the United States are Meharry graduates.

In the book, Johnson shares "his knowledge of the people and his recollection of experiences at Meharry Medical College from the forty-plus years he was there, and before and beyond.

"Johnson has revealed the remarkable and unique evolution of Meharry, a college whose spirit includes a sence of belonging to a greater whole,"according to promotional literature about the book.

"The spirit of a place is the core of its existence — it emerges from a set of vague attitudes created by the impact of different occurrences and distinct individuals. Dr. Johnson presents personalized stories about salient events and participating players, all relating to the life history of a unique school of higher learning — Meharry Medical College."

Johnson was a native of Ennis and is the son-in-law of Robert S. Shavers and Laura Garland Shavers of the Garland Community.

He received his bachelor's degree in biology from Prairie View A&M University and his master's degree from the University of Southern California. In 1947, the Johnsons moved from Los Angeles to Nashville, when Johnson became an instructor at Meharry.

Johnson attended school while he taught and earned his medical degree in 1953 from Meharry. He went on to become an assistant professor, an associate professor, the head of the biology department.

Johnson later served as academic dean of the graduate school and dean of graduate studies until 1981.

He then served as Meharry's first vice president for research and as interim dean in the School of Medicine before retiring as vice president of academic affairs and executive vice president.

"He was always a joy to be around," his wife recalled. "He loved people and being with them, especially young people. He shared his knowledge with others and didn't mind telling you what he thought about medicine."

Johnson and his wfie, Mattie, would spend a lot of time at church, visiting, vacationing and sharing their experiences in the Garland Community with family and friends.

The couple had three children: Charles W. Johnson Jr., Phillip N. Johnson and Livette S. Johnson.

Mrs. Johnson said she was grateful to all who helped her as the book was being published and especially to her sister, Jenna Benton, for helping arrange and suggest an interview with the *DeKalb News*.

A PERSON OF INFLUENCE IN THE COMMUNITY

Texarkana's Only Pulitzer Prize Winner by Jerry Atkins

Scott Joplin was a master composer of classic ragtimeHe was one of the iInfluential American Figures in the formation of twentieth century music. Ragtime was a contemporary of the earliest jazz but a separate body of music. If influenced such great composers as Debussy and Stravinsky to write their own interpretations of ragtime music. Both jazz and ragtime are considered American original art forms.

The exact date and place of Joplin's birth is not known with certainty. We know he was born in Texas and probably in the northeast part since the U.S. Census of July 1870 locates him here in Texarkana as a two-year-old child. Historical documents lead to a date of birth as being between June 1867 and mid January 1868, Scott's parents were Giles Joplin of North Carolina and Florence Givens Joplin of Kentucky. Scott had three brothers and two sisters.

Scott attended Orr School, the a two-story structure that is now a one-story building located at 831 Laurel. It is currently used as a Community Center and Day Care Center.

The family was very musical and Scott was exposed to the piano at an early age. Almost all accountings of his early life mention a German music teacher whose name was now known to be Julius Weiss.

Scott departed Texarkana in his late teens with his two brothers, Will and Robert, headed for the Midwest. The third Brother Monroe, lived out his life in Texarkana. Two grand nieces ofScott's still live in Texarkana and another in California. These are the closest living blood descendants of Scott Joplin.

After departing Texarkana, Scott did some playing in Texas and Missoouri and traveled to St. Louis in about 1855. In 1891, newspapers reported he was back in Texarkana with a minstrel group. There was a migration of musicians to Chicago in 1893 for the World's Columbian Exposition. It was after this that he made the move to Sedalia, which was on the route, of the railroad being built between St. Louis and Kansas City. He sang with his popular vocal group known as the Texas Medley Quartette. When not traveling, he was playing on the piano in sedalia, mostly at the Maple Leaf Club.

All of the Joplins were living at the time of the publication of the famous MAPLE LEAF RAG in 1899. It has been stated that it sold over a million copies but that was over a long period of time. It allowed him liberation from the roll of being just a saloon piano player. He moved to St. Louis in 1901, with his new wife, Belle Hayden. Many of Joplin's most important rags were published in those St. Louis years. After his marriage to Belle came to an end, Scott returned to Arkansas in 1904 and married Freddie Alexander in Little Rock. Unfortunately, he new wife died of pneumonia ten weeks later. After the funeral, Scott left Sedalia, never to return.

There is strong evidence that he was working on his new opera TREMONISHA with Freddie in mind. Scott had parted company with his long time Sedalia publisher, John Stark and went to New York to try to get help from many important people. Fortunately, there was a renewal of his friendship with Stark, who published many new Joplin rags.

Even though non of Scott's music was written while living in Texarkana, he never forgot about his early musical heritage. His heart and soul still remained in the Red River Valley and the dense forests of Northeast Texas and Sooutthwest Arkansas. He stated that the setting of the opera was about 10 miles north of Texarkana. One historian believes that his second wife from Arkansas was his inspiration for the main character, TREEMONISHA. It's story takes place in 1884 and relates to how education can overcome radical inequality. Despite many efforts, there were only some fragmented performances of portions of the opera. Joplin never saw a completed staged performance.

Disappointment and frustration began to take its toll. He spent some time in a hospital from long developing physical problems. He was transferred to a mental institution where he died on April 1917. Reports of a large funderal procession are pure fiction. He was almost a forgotten man when he died. His burial in an unmarked grave was finally acknowledged by the American Society of Composers, Authors and Publishers in October 1974. A brief service at the gravesite in St. Michael's Cemetery in Astoria, Queens was held and the new bronze marker reads simply "Scott Joplin, American Composer."

1971 and 1972 were the revival years of Scott and his ragtime music. Articles appeared in important magazines and he was acclaimed as a "Genius Rediscovered." Stories of his life appeared on television, movies and many record companies were quick to record his music. An Oscar winning movie, "The Sting," certainly capitalized on the use of his music that is now mostly in the public domain. Later in 1971, the Lincoln Center Music Library performed some of hispiano music. The first complete performance of TREEMONISHA took place in Atlanta in January 1972. Later it was performed in Houston and on Broadway.

Scott Joplin was posthumously awarded "A Pulitzer Prize Special Award" for his contribution to American Music on May 3, 1976. A mural honoring this "King of Ragtime Composers" may be seen at the corner of 3rd and Main Streets in Texarkana, Texas

Source: East Texas Toourism Guide 2004, page 31

*Scott Joplin's great great niece was married to the author's paternal first cousin, Lono Johnson.

Texarkana's Only Pulitzer Prize Winner

Wright Patman

Wright Patman was a state representative and is included in the book because he was helpful in securing scholarships for deserving students who entered college after high school. If one had earned a good grade point average at the end of high school, he/she could write to Wright Patman and most likely receive tuition for matriculation in the school of one's choice. My mother contacted Wright Patman after my graduation from Garland High School, and I was able to receive a scholarship at Mary Allen Jr., College; it was the beginning of my secondary education and my growth to higher learning. A lake is name in his honor which is located between New Boston and Texarkana. I think of him each time I am in the area when I visit my home of birth. Without this scholarship I probably would never be able to have advanced thus far educationally.

Laura Pearl

Second oldest daughter of Laura V. Garland-Shavers was Laura Pearl Shavers Sands; named for her mother Laura and Laura's best friend in college (Bishop College), Pearl Alexander. My mother spoke often of her friend and sometimes they exchanged letters. Laura Pearl (Pearl) had many talents. She cared very deeply for us. She fed, clothed, taught, played, reprimanded, cooked, cleaned and even served my mother as a breast pump, nursing her when she became so uncomfortable with swollen breasts. We depended on her for everything. Oh! How we loved her!

Landon Cabell Garland -1810-1895
First Chancellor, Vanderbilt University-1875-1893

Biographical information taken from—

"Sketch of Landon Cabell Garland" by his granddaughter,
Caroline Garland Lewis Montgomery "to assist Miss Dowles in her biography"
Born: "The Grove" (plantation in Nelson County, VA
Died: 2/12/1895, Vanderbilt University, Nashville, TN

Parents: Spotswood Garland and Lucinda Rose Garland. Spotswood was lawyer and clerk of the Court of Nelson Co., VA
Grandparents: Capt. James Garland and Anne Wingfield Garland. James was captain in Revolutionary War
Grandparents: Hugh Jordan and Caroline Matilda Jordan. Hugh was a native of VA member of Amherst County Committee of Safety (1774-1775), High Sheriff, County Lieutenant, member of House of Delegates (1786-1791).
Great Grandparents: Rev. Robert Rose and Anne Fitzhugh Rose. Robert was a native of Wester Alvis, Scotland and a descendant of the ancient house of Kilravock. They moved to Essex County, VA.

Married: 1st wife, **Anne Burwell**, who only lived short while. No children
2nd wife, **Louisa Frances** (d. 1889). She was his third cousin, being the daughter of **David Garland** and **Jane Meredith Garland**. (Jane Meredith was the daughter of Jane Henry, who was the sister of Patrick Henry)

Children: **Spotswood** (died in infancy; buried in Amherst County, VA)
William Henry (died at age 17)
Lucinda Rose, who married **Burwell B. Lewis**. She, along with her four younger daughters, lived with Chancellor Garland on the Vanderbilt campus following her mother's death in 1889

(One of Lucinda's younger daughters was **Louise Garland Lewis**, who was later connected to Agnes Scott College in Decatur, GA. It was Louise Garland Lewis, who painted the portrait of Chancellor Garland which now hands in Kirkland Hall on the Vanderbilt campus.)

Three older daughters of Lucinda Rose Lewis:

Lizzie, married **Louis T. Bradfield** (Birmingham, AL)
Caroline, married **John Alexander Montgomery** (Birmingham, AL)
Rose, married **Robert Eden Scott Rives** (VA)
Maurice Hamner (engineer, Lynchburg, VA)
Twin: **Louise,** married **Dr. Milton W. Humphries**
Twin: **Landonia** (died in youth)

Jane Henry ("Jennie"), married **Dr. Eugene Allen Smith**

Annie, married **Dr. Robert Fulton**
Caroline Matilda (No information)
Alice Virginia (died at age 16)

Lankford Hall Vanderbilt University
Nashville, TN 37240
Office of the Executive Vice Chancellor for Public Affairs
405 Kirkland Hall

NOTE: A member of the Garland clan from London

FINAL STATEMENT

In my lifetime I have witnessed the metamorphosis of many of Ruth's descendants. They are servants of God and the communities in which they live – a credit to their forefathers and mothers and the roots from which they sprang.

CHANGE IN TERMS OF TIME

Of all the things we think we see
Above the quantum crest
There's more swirling in the depths of time
That no one can fathom or be

One cannot measure time
In terms of day and night
For time is only a fragment of breath
Heaved from the breast of you and me

So let us all be content to find
Ourselves, among the particles of mist
For we can only hope and risk
Time to await our own design

Yes, from His cyrsalis, we have come
Flitting our wings from flower to flower
And changing of each hour
Has taken us away to another bough

ABOUT THE AUTHOR, CO-AUTHOR AND CONTRIBUTING AUTHORS

MATTIE SHAVERS JOHNSON, a fourth generation descendent of Ruth Garland was born in DeKalb, TX, the eighth child (twin to Millie O. Shavers Collins) born to Robert S. and Laura Garland Shavers.

After publishing three books of poetry, contributing author to two others and publishing "The Spirit of a Place, called Meharry" by Charles W. Johnson, Sr. MD, now brings a documentary about the community in which she was born and its inhabitants along with the co-authors, contributing authors, memories and voices of love.

Mrs. Johnson has lived in Nashville, Tennessee since 1947. Her academic degrees include: Bachelor of Science, Tennessee State University; Master of Science, Hunter College, New York City; and Master of Science in Public Health, Meharry Medical College, Nashville, Tennessee. She was a public School teacher and college teacher for many years.

Mrs. Johnson hopes to complete and publish her next three books: "We Shall Come Rejoicing," "Abused Children," and "Lullabies for Small Children by 2016. She credits her late sisters, mother, teachers and the loving support of her family for the driving force behind her writing. She devotes her time exclusively to writing, gardening and volunteer work. Mrs. Johnson and her late husband, Charles W. Johnson, Sr., M.D. are the parents of three adult children, Charles W., Phillip N., and Livette Suzanne and one grandson, Phillip Michael.

JENNA SHAVERS BENTON

(Texas Queen – Future Farmers of America)

Benton is the youngest daughter of Laura Garland Shavers and Robert S. Shavers, the widow of Barmers Glen Benton. She is the mother of two sons and two grandsons. Benton has a B.S. from Prairie View State University with extra work toward a M.S. in Home Economics. She also studied art at Tennessee State University. She loves to design, courtier, purchase and dress impeccably. Mrs. Benton, as she is fondly addressed, accolades include Texas Queen in her early years, and travel to Universities to represent her community (Garland), from DeKalb, Texas to Tallahassee, Florida A&M.

She has received awards from her school where she taught for 14 years. Benton now enjoys collecting history from her place of birth Garland Community DeKalb, Texas and contributing her experience to pass on to others.

JAMES A. PULLIAM MEMORIAL LECTURER

RAYNARD S. KINGTON, MD, PHD
DEPUTY DIRECTOR
NATIONAL INSTITUTES OF HEALTH

Dr. Raynard S. Kington was appointed Deputy Director of the National Institutes of Health (NIH) as of February 9, 2003. The Deputy Director, NIH, functions as the Principal Deputy Director to the Director, NIH; and shares in the overall leadership, policy direction, and coordination of NIH biomedical research and research training programs of NIH's 27 Institutes and Centers. Prior to this appointment, he had been Associate Director of NIH for Behavioral and Social Sciences Research since September 2000. In addition to this role, from January 2002 to November 2002, he served as acting director of the National Institute on Alcohol Abuse and Alcoholism. Prior to coming to NIH, Dr. Kington was Director of the Division of Health Examination Statistics at the National Center for Health Statistics (NCHS) of the Centers for Disease Control and Prevention (CDC). As Division Director, he also served as Director of the National Health and Nutrition Examination Survey (NHANES), one of the nation's largest studies to assess the health of the American people. Prior to coming to NCHS, he was a Senior Scientist in the Health Program at the RAND, Dr. Kington was a Co-Director of the Drew/RAND Center on Health and Aging, a National Institute on Aging Exploratory Minority Aging Center.

Dr. Kington attended the University of Michigan, where he received his B.S. with distinction and his M.D. He subsequently completed his residency in Internal Medicine at Michael Reese Medical Center in Chicago. He was then appointed a Robert Wood Johnson Clinical Scholar at the University of Pennsylvania. While at the University of Pennsylvania, he completed his M.B.A. with distinction and his Ph.D. with concentration in Health Policy and Economic at the Wharton School and was awarded a Fontaine Fellowship. He is board-certified in Internal Medicine and Public Health and Preventive Medicine.

Dr. Kington's research has focused on the role of social factors, especially socioeconomic status, as determinants of health. His current research includes studies of the health and socioeconomic status of black immigrants, differences in populations in willingness to participate in genetic research, and racial and ethnic differences in infectious disease rates. His research has included studies of the relationship between wealth and health status; the health status of U.S. Hispanic populations; the determinants of health care services utilization; the economic impact of health care expenditures among the elderly; and racial and ethnic differences in the use of long-term care.

Iverson Edwin Shavers

- Born: October 20, 1917 in DeKalb to Robert and Laura Garland Shavers
- Attended public school at the Garland Community School
- Attended Texas College earning a Bachelor's Degree in History
- Taught public school for two months in Almount Community (near New Boston) as a relief teach for his brother Jim
- Worked at River Army Depot for about six months prior to joining the military
- Volunteered for military service in the U.S. Army Air Corps August 6, 1942
- Attended Officer Candidate School and was subsequently commissioned into the Officer Corps as a Second Lieutenant in the Quartermaster Corps. He later transferred into the Transportation Corps
- Met Pauline Cookman in Germany and married her in 1947
- Served for 20 years, retiring September 30, 1962 at the rank of Lieutenant Colonel
- His last assignment was as Professor of Military Science, Reserve Officer Training Course (ROTC) at Southern University, Baton Rouge, Louisiana
- Decorations included: Army Campaign Medal, National Defense Service Medal, World War II Victor Medal, and the Army Commendation medal with device
- Assignments included Germany, France, Korea, Port of New York City, Southern University, Baton Rouge, Louisiana
- Returned to DeKalb, Texas to take up ranching
- Adopted, along with his wife, two children: Michael Edwin and Frances Louise
- Volunteered with several community organizations
- Served on DeKalb School Board for more than 20 years, including a period as the President of the Board
- Served on the Oak Grove (Texas) Water Board for more than 20 years
- Served on the Parish Council of St. Mary's Catholic Church in New Boston, Texas

www.ingramcontent.com/pod-product-compliance
Lightning Source LLC
Chambersburg PA
CBHW061118010526
44112CB00024B/2906
9780986277184